The causes of the English Revolution 1529-1642

Lawrence Stone

Professor of History, Princeton University

Routledge & Kegan Paul

London

First published 1972
by Routledge & Kegan Paul Ltd
Broadway House, 68–74 Carter Lane
London EC4V 5EL
Printed in Great Britain by
Redwood Press Limited
Trowbridge, Wiltshire
Reprinted 1973
© Lawrence Stone 1972

ISBN 0 7100 7248 1 (c)
ISBN 0 7100 7249 x(p)

To my students and colleagues at Princeton, under whose friendly but relentless criticism these ideas have taken shape

Contents

Acknowledgments

The ideas which this book contains have been developed and modified as a result of exposure to criticism in my graduate seminar over several years, and of many conversations and one formal session with my professional colleagues. Although my students and colleagues can in no way be held responsible for the result, the finished product undoubtedly owes much to the practice of free and frank scholarly communication and criticism which takes place in the Princeton History Department. I am also, as usual, deeply indebted to my wife for constructive suggestions about both style and content.

In subtle ways, of all of which I am probably not fully conscious, I have also been influenced by my experience of revolutionary outbreaks in the contemporary world. As a passive observer of 'les évènements de mai' in Paris in 1968, and as an active participant in the crisis triggered off at Princeton by the invasion of Cambodia in May 1970, I have learned much about the nature and process of revolutions. In particular I have been made aware of the electric atmosphere of a revolutionary occasion, the drunken sense of euphoria, the belief in the limitless possibilities of improvement in the human condition. I have also been persuaded of the critical importance of the response of those in authority in determining whether or not the revolutionary mood will lead to physical violence and destruction, or to peaceful accommodation and constructive adjustment.[1]

For financial support in the preparation of this, I am grateful to the National Science Foundation (Grant GS1559X) and to the Princeton University Research Fund.

[1] L. Stone, 'Two cheers for the university', *New York Review of Books*, 22 August 1968; 'Princeton in the nation's service', *New York Review of Books*, 18 June 1970.

Preface

Early versions of all three of the chapters in this book have already been published. 'Theories of revolution' appeared in *World Politics XVIII*, 1966; 'The social origins' in my *Social Change and Revolution in England, 1540–1640*, Longmans, 1965; and 'The causes of the English Revolution' in *Preconditions of Revolution in Early Modern Europe*, ed. R. Foster and J. P. Greene, Johns Hopkins University Press, 1970. The first two have been brought up to date by the inclusion of references to more recent publications, and the last has been more than doubled in size and many of its conclusions substantially revised in the light of further experience, discussion and reflection. The first examines the theoretical models, some elements of which have been used to organize the specific historical interpretation; the second deals with the historiography of the central issue which has concerned students of this problem for the past thirty years; and the last attempts to formulate a synoptic causal analysis of why the English Revolution occurred. Despite the fact that the Revolution has been written about again and again by historians from the days of Clarendon, and despite the fact that it is recognized as a critical episode in modern English history, it is a curious fact that it is very hard to find a succinct account of just why it happened. The widely varying viewpoints of historians have to be deduced from their passing comments and their selection of the facts with which they have constructed their narrative stories. This volume is severely analytical and deliberately avoids the narrative form, except at the very end when the sequence of events clearly determined the outcome. It consequently lays itself wide open to criticism from those who believe that the historian's duty is to tell a story as truthfully and as artistically as he can, and that causal explanations in history are philosophically unsound. In fact, however, the main thing which distinguishes the narrative from the analytical historian is that the former works within a framework of models and assumptions of which he is not always fully conscious, while the latter is aware of what he is doing, and says so explicitly.

In some ways this book is an attempt to make amends for a deficiency in my previous writings which critics and friends have frequently pointed out. By focusing so narrowly on the social aspects of the historical process, they say that I have unduly neglected the religious, political, administrative, and constitutional elements of the story and that I have given the impression that I thought they did not matter. I confess that I still regard formal constitutional history treated *in vacuo* (as it was, and perhaps still is, in many English universities) as one of the most sterile and meaningless ways of cutting into the tangled thickets of historical change. From their very different perspectives, both Karl Marx and Walter Bagehot were agreed on that point.

But politics, meaning the nature, ownership and degree of power exercised in the society, is central to any historical development, particularly of an organized nation state with a long history behind it, like England. Nor can there be any doubt that administrative institutions, once created, take on a life of their own, and may become exceedingly impervious and unresponsive to calls for change in function or organization. To ignore the administrative role of the central government, the numerous local governmental agencies, the churches, the educational institutions or the army is thus to miss a critically important area of the total historical experience. In this book an attempt has been made to deal with these broader perspectives within which, and only within which, the findings of the social historians can properly be understood. The justification for including a special chapter on the social origins of the revolution is not that this is the most important set of causes, much less the only one, but that it is the one which has generated most research and dispute over the last generation.

The period and the various aspects of the problem have been subjected to the most extensive inquiry during the last thirty years, more intensive, perhaps, than for any other phase of English history. The moment seems right, therefore, to stand back and try to see the forest as a whole rather than the individual trees. My indebtedness to the numerous and distinguished scholars in the field will be apparent from the footnotes, even if not all of them will be entirely happy with the conclusions I have drawn from their researches. This is a battle-ground which has been heavily fought over, and is beset with mines, booby-traps and ambushes manned by ferocious scholars prepared to fight every inch of the way. This highly personal interpretation is therefore unlikely to meet with general acceptance. But the intention is not to propound a definitive solùtion, but rather to offer one scholar's inevitably imperfect version of why things happened the way they did. If this little book acts as a stimulus to further and more methodologically sophisticated debate, it will have served its purpose.

'If the revolution has triumphed so quickly, it is exclusively because, as a result of an absolutely new historical situation, a number of completely different currents, a number of completely heterogeneous class interests, and a number of completely opposite social and political tendencies have become fused into one with remarkable coherence.'

(Lenin, quoted by L. Althuser, *Pour Marx*, Paris, 1965, p. 98, n. 2)

'Revolution is not a discrete, relatively isolable, purely political phenomenon; the factors that contribute to it are as manifold as the elements comprising society itself.'

(Chalmers Johnson, *Revolutionary Change*, Boston, 1966, p. xi)

Part 1

Historiography

Chapter 1

Theories of revolution

In attacking the problem of revolution, as most others of major significance in history, we historians should think twice before we spurn the help offered by our colleagues in the social sciences, who have, as it happens, been particularly active in the last few years in theorizing about the typology, causes, and evolutionary patterns of this particular phenomenon. The purpose of this chapter is not to advance any new hypothesis, but to provide a summary view and critical examination of the work that has been going on.

The first necessity in any inquiry is a careful definition of terms: what is, and what is not, a revolution? According to one view, it is change effected by the use of violence in government, and/or regime, and/or society.[1] By *society* is meant the consciousness and the mechanics of communal solidarity, which may be tribal, peasant, kinship, national, and so on; by *regime* is meant the constitutional structure – democracy, oligarchy, monarchy; and by *government* is meant specific political and administrative institutions. Violence, it should be noted, is not the same as force; it is force used with un-necessary intensity, unpredictably, and usually destructively.[2] This definition of revolution is a very broad one, and two historians of the French Revolution, Crane Brinton and Louis Gottschalk, would prefer to restrict the use of the word to the major political and social upheavals with which they are familiar, the 'Great Revolutions', as George S. Pettee calls them.[3]

Even the wider definition allows the historian to distinguish between, on the one hand, the seizure of power that leads to a major restructuring of government or society, the establishment of a new set of values for distributive justice, and the replacement of the former élite by a new one, and on the other hand, the *coup d'état* involving no more than a change of ruling personnel by violence or threat of violence. This latter is the norm in Latin America, where it occurred thirty-one times in the ten years 1945–55. Merle Kling has arrived at a suggestive explanation of this Latin American pheno-menon of chronic political instability, limited but frequent use of violence, and almost complete lack of social or institutional change. He argues that ownership of the principal economic resources, both agricultural and mineral, is concentrated in the hands of a tiny, very stable, élite of enormously wealthy monoculture landlords and mining capitalists. This élite is all-powerful and cannot be attacked by opposition groups within the country; externally, however, it is dependent on foreign interests for its markets and its capital. In this colonial situation of a foreign-supported, closed plutocracy, the main avenue of rapid upward social mobility for non-members of the élite leads, via the army, to the capture of the government machine, which is the only accessible source of wealth and power. This political instability is permitted by the élite on the condition that its own interests are undisturbed. Instability, limited violence, and the absence of social or institutional change are therefore all the product of the contradiction between the realities of a colonial economy run by a plutocracy and the façade of political sovereignty – between the real, stable power of the economic élite and the nominal, unstable control of politicians and generals.[4]

The looser definition of revolution thus suits both historians of major social change and historians of the palace *coup*. It does, however, raise certain difficulties. First, there is a wide range of changes of government by violence which are neither a mere substitution of personalities in positions of power nor a prelude to the restructuring of society; second, conservative counter-revolutions become almost impossible to fit into the model; and last, it remains hard to distinguish between colonial wars, civil wars, and social revolution.

To avoid these difficulties, an alternative formulation has recently been put forward by a group of social scientists working mainly at Princeton. They have dropped the word 'revolution' altogether and put 'internal war' in its place.[5] This is defined as any attempt to alter state policy, rulers, or institutions by the use of violence in societies where violent competition is not the norm and where well-defined institutional patterns exist.[6] This concept seems to be a logical consequence of the preoccupation of sociologists in recent years with a model of society in a stable, self-regulating state of perpetual equipoise. In this utopian world of universal harmony all forms of violent conflict are anomalies, to be treated alike as pathological disorders of a similar species. This is a model which, although it has its uses for analytical purposes, bears little relation to the reality familiar to the historian. It looks to a society without change, with universal consensus on values, with complete social harmony, and isolated from external threats; no approximation to such a society has ever been seen.

The crude opposite model is based on pure interest theory and postulates that the social order rests on physical coercion of the majority by a minority in order to distribute material rewards and power in an inequitable way. The state claims a monopoly of violence, and the consequent suppression of internal disorder is its *raison d'être*. Societies become unstable only because the relation between authority and force becomes unstable. It is obvious that this model bears no more relation to reality than its opposite, since society is in fact both a moral community held together by shared values, which give the state legitimacy, and also a system of control, employing in the last resort the force necessary to prevent deviance and disorder. A more reasonable model is one which accepts that all societies are in a condition of uneasy equilibrium, whose stability is always threatened by a host of political conflicts, but which is usually held in balance partly by social norms and ideological beliefs and partly by physical sanctions.[7] Instability may arise from material conflicts over the distribution of scarce economic resources or political power; or from a breakdown of values due to inadequate socialization of the young, exacerbated conflict between mutually incompatible roles, or group dissensus over norms. Such conflicts are usually settled by suitable adjustment mechanisms, and it is only in rare moments that a society is sufficiently shaken to undertake major structural alterations.

The first objection to the all-embracing formula of internal war is that, by covering all forms of physical conflict from strikes and terrorism to civil war, it isolates the use of violence from the normal process of societal adjustment. Though some of the users of the term express their awareness that the use of violence for political ends is a fairly common occurrence, the definition they have established in fact excludes all times and places where it *is* common. It thus cuts out most societies the world has ever known, including Western Europe in the middle ages and Latin America today. Second, it isolates one particular means, physical violence, from the political ends that it is designed to serve. Clausewitz's famous definition of external war is equally applicable to internal war, civil war, or revolution: 'War is not only a political act, but a real political instrument; a continuation of political transactions, an accomplishment of them by different means. That which remains peculiar to war relates only to the peculiar nature of its means.'[8]

It is perfectly true that any means by which society exercises pressure or control, whether it is administrative organization, constitutional law, economic interest or physical force, can be a fruitful field of study in its own right, so long as its students remain aware that they are looking at only one part of a larger whole. It is also true that there is something peculiar about violence, if only because of man's highly ambivalent attitude towards the killing of his own species. Somehow he regards physical force as different in kind from, say, economic exploitation or psychological manipulation as a means of exercising power over others. But this distinction is not one of much concern to the historian of revolution, in which violence is a normal and natural occurrence. The concept of internal war is too broad in its comprehension of all types of violence from civil wars to strikes, too narrow in its restriction to normally non-violent societies, too limited in its concern with one of many means, too arbitrary in its separation of this means from the ends in view, and too little concerned with the complex roots of social unrest to be of much practical value to him.

The most fruitful typology of revolution is that of Chalmers Johnson, set out in a pamphlet that deserves to be widely read.[9] He sees six types, identified by the targets selected for attack, whether the government personnel, the political regime, or the community as a social unit; by the nature of the carriers of revolution, whether a mass or an élite; and particularly by the goals and the ideologies, whether reformist, eschatological, nostalgic, nation-forming, élitist or nationalist. The first type, the *jacquerie*, is a spontaneous mass peasant rising, usually carried out in the name of the traditional authorities, Church and King, and with the limited aims of purging the local or national élites. Examples are the English Peasant Revolt of 1381, Kett's Rebellion in Norfolk of 1549, and the Pugachev Rebellion in Russia in 1773–5. The second type, the *millenarian rebellion*, is similar to the first but with the added feature of a utopian dream, inspired by a living messiah. This type can be .found at all times, in all parts of the world, from the Florentine Revolution led by Savonarola in 1494, to the Anabaptist rebellion in Munster led by John Mathijs and John Beukels in 1533–1535, to the Sioux Ghost-Dance Rebellion inspired by the Paiute prophet, Wovoka, in 1890. It has attracted a good deal of attention from historians in recent years, partly because the career of Hitler offered overwhelming proof of the enormous historical significance of a charismatic leader, and partly because of a growing interest in the ideas of Max Weber.[10] The third type is the *anarchistic rebellion*, the nostalgic reaction to progressive change, involving a romantic idealization of the old order; the Pilgrimage of Grace and the Vendée are examples of this.

The fourth is that very rare phenomenon, the *Jacobin Communist revolution*. This type of revolution can occur only in a highly centralized state with good communications and a large capital city, and its target is government, regime, and society – the lot. The result is likely to be the creation of a new national consciousness under centralized, military authority, a re-distribution of property and authority, and the erection of a more rational, and hence more efficient, social and bureaucratic order on the ruins of the old ramshackle structure of privilege, nepotism, and corruption.

The fifth type is the *conspiratorial coup d'état*, the planned work of a tiny élite fired by an oligarchic, sectarian ideology. This qualifies as a revolutionary type only if it in fact anticipates a mass movement and inaugurates social change – for example, the Nasser Revolution in Egypt or the Castro Revolution in Cuba; it is thus clearly distinguished from the palace revolt, assassination, dynastic succession-conflict, strike, banditry, and other forms of violence, which are all subsumed under the 'internal war' rubric.

Finally, there is the *militarized mass insurrection*, a new phenomenon of the twentieth century in that it is a deliberately planned mass revolutionary war, guided by a dedicated élite. The outcome of guerilla warfare is determined by political attitudes, not military strategy or material, for the rebels are wholly dependent on broad popular support. In all cases on record the ideology that attracts the mass following has been a combination of xenophobic nationalism and Marxism, with by far the greater stress on the former. This type of struggle has occurred in Yugoslavia, China, Algeria, and Vietnam.

Although, like any schematization of the historical process, this six-fold typology is concerned with ideal types, and although in practice individual revolutions may sometimes display characteristics of several different types, the fact remains that this is much the most satisfactory classification we have so far; it is one that working historians can recognize and use with profit. The one obvious criticism is semantic, an objection to the use of the phrase 'Jacobin Communist revolution'.[11] Some of Johnson's examples are Communist, such as the Russian or Chinese Revolutions; others are Jacobin but not Communist, such as the French Revolution or the

Turkish Revolution of 1908–22. It would be better to revert to Pettee's category of 'Great Revolutions', and treat Communist revolutions as a sub-category, one type, but not the only type, of the modernizing revolutionary process.

Given this classification and definition of revolution, what are its root causes? Here everyone is agreed in making a sharp distinction between long-run, underlying causes – the preconditions, which create a potentially explosive situation and can be analysed on a comparative basis – and immediate, incidental factors – the precipitants, which trigger the outbreak and which may be non-recurrent, personal, and fortuitous. This effectively disposes of the objections of those historians whose antipathy to conceptual schematization takes the naïve form of asserting the uniqueness of each historical event.

One of the first in the field of model-building was Crane Brinton, who as long ago as 1938 put forward a series of uniformities common to the four great Western revolutions: English, French, American, and Russian. These included an economically advancing society, growing class and status antagonisms, an alienated intelligentsia, a psychologically insecure and politically inept ruling class, and a governmental financial crisis.[12]

The subjectivity, ambiguity, and partial self-contradiction of this and other analyses of the causes of specific revolutions – for example the French Revolution – have been cruelly shown up by Harry Eckstein.[13] He has pointed out that commonly adduced hypotheses run the spectrum of particular conditions, moving from the intellectual (inadequate political socialization, conflicting social myths, a corrosive social philosophy, alienation of the intellectuals) to the economic (increasing poverty, rapid growth, imbalance between production and distribution, long-term growth plus short-term recession) to the social (resentment due to restricted élite circulation, confusion due to excessive élite recruitment, anomie due to excessive social mobility, conflict due to the rise of new social classes) to the political (bad government, divided government, weak government, oppressive government). Finally there are explanations on the level of general process, such as rapid social change, erratic social change, or a lack of harmony between the state structure and society, the rulers and the ruled. None of these explanations are invalid in themselves, but they are often difficult or impossible to reconcile one with the other, and are so diverse in their range and variety as to be virtually impossible to fit into an ordered, analytical framework. What, then, is to be done?

Fundamental to all analyses, whether by historians like Brinton and Gottschalk or by political scientists like Johnson and Eckstein, is the recognition of a lack of harmony between the social system on the one hand and the political system on the other. This situation Johnson calls *dysfunction*, a word derived from the structural-functional equilibrium model of the sociologists. This dysfunction may have many causes, some of which are merely random or cyclical, such as may develop because of personal weaknesses in hereditary kingships or single-party regimes. In these cases, the revolution will not take on serious proportions, and will limit itself to attacks on the governing élite, or at most the governing institutions, leaving regime and society intact. In most cases, however, including all those of real importance, the dysfunction is the result of some new and developing process, as a result of which certain social sub-systems find themselves in a condition of relative deprivation. Rapid economic growth, imperial conquest, new metaphysical beliefs, and important technological changes are the four commonest factors involved, in that order. If the process of change is sufficiently slow and sufficiently moderate, the dysfunction may not arise to dangerous levels. Alternatively, the élite may adjust to the new situation with sufficient rapidity and skill to ride out the storm and retain popular confidence. But if the change is rapid and profound, it may cause the sense of deprivation, alienation and anomie and spread into many sectors of society at once, causing what Johnson calls multiple dysfunction, which may be all but incurable within the existing political system.

In either case the second vital element in creating a revolutionary situation is the condition and attitude of the entrenched élite, a factor on which Eckstein rightly lays great stress. The élite may lose its manipulative skill, or its military superiority, or its self-confidence, or its cohesion; it may become estranged from the non-élite, or overwhelmed by a financial crisis; it may be incompetent, or weak or brutal. Any combination of two or more of these features will be dangerous. What is ultimately fatal, however, is the compounding of its errors by intransigence. If it fails to anticipate the need for reform, if it blocks all peaceful, constitutional means of social adjustment, then it unites the various deprived elements in single-minded opposition to it, and drives them down the narrow road to violence. It is this process of polarization into two coherent groups or alliances of what are naturally and normally a series of fractional and shifting tensions and conflicts within a society that both Peter Amman and Wilbert Moore see as the essential preliminary to the outbreak of a Jacobin revolution.[14] To conclude, therefore, revolution becomes *possible* when a condition of multiple dysfunction meets an intransigent élite: just such a conjunction occurred in the decades immediately before the English, the French, and the Russian Revolutions.

Revolution only becomes *probable* (Johnson might say 'certain'), however, if certain special factors intervene: the 'precipitants' or 'accelerators'. Of these, the three most common are the emergence of an inspired leader or prophet; the formation of a secret, military, revolutionary organization; and the crushing defeat of the armed forces in foreign war. This last is of critical importance since it not only shatters the prestige of the ruling élite, but also undermines the morale and discipline of the soldiers and thus opens the way to the violent overthrow of the existing government.

The defects of Johnson's 1964 model were partly overcome by his revision of 1966. The main defect was that it concentrated too much on objective structural conditions, and attempted to relate these conditions directly to political actions. In the new version far greater scope is allowed for ideas and values as the mediating factor between the conditions and the response. Johnson now recognizes that a social system may be upset just as much by changes in values – for example, the spread of new ideas either coming from 'marginal men' or from innovating élites – as by changes in the environment – for example, changes in industrial techniques and organization, modern medicine or foreign trade. He unnecessarily complicates his categories by sub-dividing them into exogenous and indogenous, which is largely meaningless. For what does it matter whether the technology or the idea is home grown or imported? All the same, this new emphasis on both environment and values makes it possible to explain why in the past similar political activity has occurred in different environmental conditions, and different activity in similar conditions. An approach which lays equal stress on such things as anomie, alienation of the intellectuals, frustrated popular aspirations, élite estrangement, and loss of élite self-confidence, is more likely to produce a satisfactory historical explanation than is one that sticks to the objective social situation.

In his later book Johnson goes far to remedy the second major defect of his 1964 model, namely its determinist neglect of the role of the unique and the personal. He seemed to regard his accelerators as automatic triggers, ignoring the area of unpredictable personal choice that is always left to the ruling élite and to the revolutionary leaders, even in a situation of multiple dysfunction exacerbated by an accelerator. Revolution is never inevitable – or rather the only evidence of its inevitability is that it actually happens. Consequently the only way to prove this point is to indulge in just the kind of hypothetical argument that historians prudently try to avoid. Thus it is still just possible that modernization may take place in Morocco and India without revolution. The modernization and industrialization of Germany and Britain took place without revolution in the nineteenth century (though it can be argued that in the latter case the process was slow by twentieth-century standards, and that, as is now becoming all too apparent, the modernization was far from complete). Some think that a potentially revolutionary situation in the United States in the 1930s was avoided by shrewd political action. In his 1966 model Johnson recognized the role of the personality as a semi-independent variable in the social system, free to operate within the limits roped off and labelled 'crime' or 'mental sickness'.

One of the unresolved difficulties of the Johnson model is that it makes no allowance for the fact that political actions taken to remedy dysfunction often precipitate change themselves. This produces the paradoxical hypothesis that measures designed to restore equilibrium in fact upset equilibrium. Because he begins with his structural-functional equilibrium model, Johnson is a victim of the fallacy of intended consequences. As often as not in history it is the *unintended* consequences that really matter: to mention but one example, it was Louis XVI's belated and half-hearted attempts at reform that provoked the aristocratic reaction, which in turn opened the way to the bourgeois, the peasant, and the sans-culotte revolutions. Finally the dysfunction concept is not altogether easy to handle in a concrete historical case. If societies are regarded as being in a constant state of multiple tension, then some degree of dysfunction is always present. Some group is always in a state of relative deprivation due to the inevitable process of social change.

Recognition of this fact leads Eckstein to point out the importance of forces working *against* revolution. Historians, particularly those formed in the Western liberal tradition, are reluctant to admit that ruthless efficient repression – as opposed to bumbling, half-hearted repression – involving the physical destruction of leading revolutionaries and effective control of the media of communication, can crush incipient revolutionary movements. Repression is particularly effective when governments know what to look for, when they have before their eyes the unfortunate example of other governments overthrown by revolutionaries elsewhere. Reaction, in fact, is just as infectious as revolution. Moreover, diversion of energy and attention to successful – as opposed to unsuccessful – foreign war can ward off serious internal trouble. Quietist – as opposed to activist – religious movements may serve as the opiate of the people, as Halévy suggested about Methodism in England. Bread and circuses may distract popular attention. Timely – as opposed to untimely – political concessions may win over moderate opinion and isolate the extremists.

Basing himself on this suggestive analysis, Eckstein produces a paradigm for universal application. He sees four positive variables – élite inefficiency, disorienting social process, subversion, and available rebel facilities – and four negative variables – diversionary mechanisms, available incumbent facilities, adjustive mechanisms, and effective repression. Each type of internal war, and each step of each type, can, he suggests, be explained in terms of these eight variables. While this may be true, it is fair to point out that some of the variables are themselves the product of more deep-seated factors, others mere questions of executive action that may be determined by the accidents of personality. Disruptive social process is a profound cause; élite inefficiency a behaviour pattern; effective repression a function of will; facilities the by-product of geography. One objection to the Eckstein paradigm is therefore that it embraces different levels of explanation and fails to maintain the fundamental distinction between preconditions and precipitants. Second, it concentrates on the factors working for or against the successful manipulation of violence rather than on the underlying factors working to produce a revolutionary potential. This is because the paradigm is intended to apply to all forms of internal war rather than to revolution proper, and because all that the various forms of internal war have in common is the use of violence. It is impossible to tell how serious these criticisms are until the paradigm has been applied to a particular historical revolution. Only then will its value become apparent.

If we take the behaviourist approach, then a primary cause of revolutions is the emergence of an obsessive revolutionary mentality.

But how closely does the subjective mentality relate to the objective material circumstances? In every revolutionary situation one finds a group of men – fanatics, extremists, zealots – so convinced of their own righteousness and of the urgent need to create a new Jerusalem on earth (whether formally religious or secular in inspiration is irrelevant) that they are prepared to smash through the normal restraint of habit, custom, and convention. Such men were the seventeenth-century English Puritans, the eighteenth-century French Jacobins, the early twentieth-century Russian Bolsheviks, and the late twentieth-century Maoists in Pekin, Paris and New York. But what makes such men is far from certain. What generates such ruthlessness in curbing evil, such passion for discipline and order? Rapid social mobility, both horizontal and vertical, and particularly urbanization, certainly produces a sense of rootlessness and anxiety. In highly stratified societies even some of the newly-risen elements may find themselves under stress.[15] While some of the *arrivistes* are happily absorbed in their new strata, others remain uneasy and resentful. If they are snubbed and rebuffed by the older members of the status group to which they aspire by reason of their new wealth and position, they are likely to become acutely conscious of their social inferiority, and may be driven either to adopt a pose *plus royaliste que le roi* or to dream of destroying the whole social order. In the latter case they may try to allay their sense of insecurity by imposing their norms and values by force upon society at large. This is especially the case if there is available a moralistic ideology like Puritanism or Marxism to which they can attach themselves, and which provides them with unshakable confidence in their own rectitude.

But why does the individual react in one particular way rather than another? Some would argue that the character of the revolutionary is formed by sudden ideological conversion in adolescence or early adult life (to Puritanism, Jacobinism, or Bolshevism) as a refuge from this anxiety state.[16] What is not acceptable is the fashionable conservative cliché that the revolutionary and the reformer are merely the chance product of unfortunate psychological difficulties in childhood. It is possible that this is the mechanism by which such feelings are generated, though there is increasing evidence of the continued plasticity of human character, until at any rate post-adolescence, and of the happy and well-adjusted childhood of most of the modern radicals. In any case, this crude psychological reductionism cannot explain why some individuals respond to stress by adopting radical ideas and others live blamelessly conformist lives. The other main objection to this theory is that it fails to explain why these particular attitudes become common only in certain classes and age groups at certain times and in certain places. This failure strongly suggests that the cause of this state of mind lies not in the personal maladjustment of the individuals or their parents, but in the social conditions that created that maladjustment. Talcott Parsons treats disaffection or 'alienation' as a generalized phenomenon that may manifest itself in crime, alcoholism, drug addiction, daytime fantasies, religious enthusiasm, or serious political agitation. To use Robert Merton's formulation, ritualism and retreatism are two possible psychological escape-routes; innovation and rebellion two others.[17] Gripped by frustration generated by environmental circumstances, the individual may get drunk, beat his wife, retire to a monastery, write a book, throw a bomb, or start a revolution.

Even if we accept a generally behaviourist approach (which I do), the fact remains that many of the underlying causes both of the alienation of the revolutionaries and of the weakness of the incumbent élite are economic in origin; and it is in this area that some interesting work has centred. In particular a fresh look has been taken at the contradictory models of Marx and de Tocqueville, the one claiming that popular revolution is a product of increasing misery, the other that it is a product of increasing prosperity. Two economists, Sir Arthur Lewis and Mancur Olson, have pointed out that because of their basic social stability, both pre-industrial and highly industrialized societies are relatively free from revolutionary disturbance.[18] In the former societies people accept with little question the accepted rights and obligations of family, class, and caste. Misery, oppression, and social injustice are passively endured as inevitable features of life on earth. It is in societies experiencing rapid economic growth that the trouble usually occurs. Lewis, who is thinking mostly about the newly emerging countries, primarily of Africa, regards the sense of frustration that leads to revolution as a consequence first of the dislocation of the old status patterns by the emergence of four new classes – the proletariat, the capitalist employers, the urban commercial and professional middle class, and the professional politicians; and second of the disturbance of the old income patterns by the sporadic and patchy impact of economic growth, which creates new wealth and new poverty in close and conspicuous juxtaposition. Both phenomena he regards as merely transitional, since in a country fully developed economically there are strong tendencies toward the reduction of inequalities of opportunity, income, and status.

This model matches fairly well the only detailed analysis of a historical revolution in which a conscious effort has been made to apply modern sociological methods. In his recent study of the Vendée, Charles Tilly argues that a counter-revolutionary situation was the consequence of special tensions created by the immediate juxtaposition of, on one hand, parish clergy closely identified with the local communities, great absentee landlords and old-fashioned subsistence farming; and, on the other, a large-scale textile industry on the putting-out system and increasing bourgeois competitition.[19] Though the book is flawed by a tendency to take a ponderous sociological hammer to crack a simple little historical nut, it is none the less a suggestive and successful pioneering example of the application of new hypotheses and techniques to historical material.

Olson has independently developed a more elaborate version of the Lewis theory. He argues that revolutionaries are *déclassé* and freed from the social bonds of family, profession, village or manor; and that these individuals are the product of rapid economic growth, which creates both *nouveaux riches* and *nouveaux pauvres*. The former, usually middle-class and urban artisans, are better off economically, but are disoriented, rootless, and restless; the latter may be workers whose wages have failed to keep pace with inflation, workers in technologically outdated and therefore declining industries, or the unemployed in a society in which the old cushions of the extended family and the village have gone, and in which the new cushion of social security has not yet been created. The initial growth phase may well cause a decline in the standard of living of the majority because of the need for relatively enormous forced savings for reinvestment. The result is a revolution caused by the widening gap between expectations – social and political for the new rich, economic for the new poor – and the realities of everyday life.

A sociologist, James C. Davies, agrees with Olson that the fundamental impetus towards a revolutionary situation is generated by rapid economic growth but he associates such growth with a generally rising rather than a generally falling standard of living, and argues that the moment of potential revolution is reached only when the long-term phase of growth is followed by a short-term phase of economic stagnation or decline.[20] The result of this 'J-curve', as he calls it, is that steadily soaring expectations, newly created by the period of growth, shoot further and further ahead of actual satisfaction of needs. Successful revolution is the work neither of the destitute nor of the well-satisfied, but of those whose actual situation is improving less rapidly than they expect.

These economic models have much in common, and their differences can be explained by the fact that Lewis and Olson are primarily concerned with the long-term economic forces creating instability, and Davies with the short-term economic factors that may precipitate a crisis. Moreover their analyses apply to different kinds of economic growth, of which three have recently been identified by W. W. Rostow and Barry Supple: there is the expansion of production in a pre-industrial society, which may not cause any important technological, ideological, social, or political change; there is the phase of rapid growth, involving major changes of every kind; and there is the sustained trend towards technological maturity.[21] Historians have been quick to see that these models, particularly that of Rostow, can be applied only to a limited number of historical cases. The trouble is not so much that in any specific case the phases – particularly the last two – tend to merge into one another, but that changes in the various sectors occur at irregular and unexpected places on the time-scale in different societies. In so far as there is any validity in the division of the stages of growth into these three basic types, the revolutionary model of Olson and Lewis is confined to the second; that of Davies is applicable to all three.

The Davies model fits the history of Western Europe quite well, for it looks as if in conditions of extreme institutional and ideological rigidity the first type of economic growth may produce frustrations of a very serious kind. Revolutions broke out all over Europe in the 1640s, twenty years after a secular growth phase had come to an end.[22] C. E. Labrousse has demonstrated the existence of a similar economic recession in France from 1778,[23] and from 1914 the Russian economy was dislocated by the war effort after many years of rapid growth. Whatever its limitations in any particular situation, the J-curve of actual satisfaction of needs is an analytical tool that historians can usefully bear in mind as they probe the violent social upheavals of the past.

As de Tocqueville pointed out, this formula of advance followed by retreat is equally applicable to other sectors. Trouble arises if a phase of liberal governmental concessions is followed by a phase of political repression; a phase of fairly open recruitment channels into the élite followed by a phase of aristocratic reaction and a closing of ranks; a phase of weakening status barriers by a phase of reassertion of privilege. The J-curve is applicable to other than purely economic satisfactions, and the apex of the curve is the point at which underlying causes, the preconditions, merge with immediate factors, the precipitants. The recipe for revolution is thus the creation of new expectations by economic improvement and some social and political reforms, followed by economic recession, governmental reaction, and aristocratic resurgence, which widen the gap between expectations and reality.

All these attempts to relate dysfunction to relative changes in economic prosperity and aspirations are hampered by two things, of which the first is the extreme difficulty in ascertaining the facts. It is never easy to discover precisely what is happening to the distribution of wealth in a given society. Even now, even in highly developed Western societies with massive bureaucratic controls and quantities of statistical data, there is no agreement about the facts. Some years ago it was confidently believed that in both Britain and the United States incomes were being levelled, and that extremes of both wealth and poverty were being steadily eliminated. Today, no one quite knows what is happening in either country.[24] And if this is true now, still more is it true of societies in the past about which the information is fragmentary and unreliable.

Second, even if they can be clearly demonstrated, economic trends are only one part of the problem. Historians are increasingly realizing that the psychological responses to changes in wealth and power are not only not precisely related to, but are politically more significant than, the material changes themselves. As Marx himself realized at one stage, dissatisfaction with the *status quo* is not determined by absolute realities but by relative expectations. 'Our desires and pleasures spring from society; we measure them, therefore, by society, and not by the objects which serve for their satisfaction. Because they are of a social nature, they are of a relative nature.'[25] Frustration may possibly result from a rise and subsequent relapse in real income. But it is perhaps more likely to be caused by a rise in aspirations that outstrips the rise in real income; or by a rise in the *relative* economic position in society of the group in question, followed by a period in which its real income continues to grow, but less fast than that of other groups around it. Alternatively it may represent a rise and then decline of status, largely unrelated to real income; or if there is a relationship between status and real income, it may be an inverse one. For example, social scientists seeking to explain the rise of the radical right in the United States in the early 1950s and again in the early 1960s attribute it to a combination of great economic prosperity and an aggravated sense of insecurity of status.[26] Whether or not this is a general formula for right-wing rather than left-wing revolutionary movements is not yet clear.

Moreover the problem is further complicated by an extension of reference-group theory.[27] Human satisfaction is related not to existing conditions but to the condition of a social group against which the individual measures his situation. In an age of mass communications and the wide distribution of cheap radio receivers, even among the impoverished illiterate of the world, knowledge of high consumption standards elsewhere spreads rapidly, and as a result the reference group may be in another, more highly developed, country or even continent. Under these circumstances revolutionary conditions may be created before industrialization has got properly under way.

All modern theories of revolutionary behaviour are based on the 'relative deprivation' hypothesis that it is generated by the gap between expectations and the perceptions of reality. The psychological chain of causation links the gap to frustration, and frustration to aggression. This is the central theme of Professor Gurr's study of revolutions.[28] Although darkened by obfuscating jargon, much of which conceals solemn statements of the obvious, although peppered with a maddening array of numbered hypotheses and corollaries, and although disfigured with bewildering charts full of boxes and arrows running every way, the book nevertheless has interesting things to say. Relative deprivation may take the form of a gap between expectations and perceived capabilities over three general sets of values: 'welfare', meaning economic conditions; political power; and social status – the three old Weberian categories. The gap may open up through *decremental deprivation*, involving stable expectations and a decline of capabilities. This may be caused by a general economic depression, or more likely by selective economic impoverishment of a specific group, for example, English hand-loom weavers in the early nineteenth century, or parish clergy in the twentieth. Or it may be caused by political repression and the exclusion of a certain group from political participation; or it may be caused by a relative status decline due to the rise of competing groups. The second type is *progressive deprivation*, in which a long period of improvement is followed by a sudden downward turn in capabilities, while expectations go on rising because of past experience. This is Davies's 'J-curve', now extended to more than merely material circumstances. The third is *aspirational deprivation*, in which expectations rise while capabilities remain the same. This is fairly rare in the past, although the Reformation may be looked at in this light, in the terms of rising lay expectations of spiritual zeal from the clergy, which the latter could not satisfy. Today it is common among under-developed countries, as populations learn about the benefits of modernization elsewhere. The intensity of the deprivation varies with the size of the gap; with the importance the group ascribes to the value affected – the poor attach most value to economic conditions, the rich to political participation; with the extent that alternative satisfactions are available; and with the duration of the existence of the gap.

The factors causing a rise of expectations are identified as urbanization, literacy, the demonstration effect of striking improvement elsewhere, new ideologies, especially of a chiliastic character, and an inconsistency between the three variables of wealth, power and status. G. Lenski has laid great emphasis on this last factor, itself a product of social mobility.[29] The upwardly mobile tend to find that their status and power are not commensurate with their wealth, since the old élites will not accept them as social equals or share power with them. The downwardly mobile retain their status for a while, but lose wealth and power. In either case the discrepancy breeds anxiety, the anxiety resentment, and the resentment aggression which may find an outlet in radical ideologies and actions. Gurr points to the 'zero-sum' aspect of the distribution of all goods. Even economic resources are valued largely in relative terms, compared with the wealth of close reference groups, and power and status are relative by definition; the more of them obtained by one person or group, the less of them is available for others. On the other hand moderation in the appetite of the élite, some modesty in the display of affluence, some restraint in its assertions of social superiority, some tolerance of élite circulation from below, all help to dampen the fires of resentment.

All this is quite helpful as far as it goes, in identifying the causes of resentment in a social system and in devising ways of assessing its intensity and spread. But Gurr is not particularly helpful on the coercive balance of physical force between élite and dissidents, or on the role of ideology, or on the complex interaction of all these factors to generate a revolution. In particular he ignores the 'X factor' of personality and choice, and his model is so mechanical and schematized as to be hard to apply to any given situation. His main contribution is his analysis of the types and causes of relative deprivation.

Another recent theory regards the 'Great Revolutions' as stages in the modernization of under-developed societies.[30] The central feature of a pre-revolutionary situation is the unwillingness or incapacity of the ruling élite to carry out the transformation needed to raise productivity, increase trade, expand education, redistribute and exploit capital resources. The principle consequence of the revolution is to strengthen the governmental machinery to carry out these tasks. The modernization theory of revolution looks suspiciously like the Marxist bourgeois revolution in a new guise. It is a theory which fits late twentieth-century revolutions in backward countries well enough, but it is difficult to accommodate the older revolutions to the model. In what ways were the pre-revolutionary governments of Charles I and Louis XVI failing in their modernization functions? In what ways were the Parliamentary leaders of 1640 or 1789 trying to innovate with this purpose in mind? The recent stress on the political and modernizing aspects of the causes and consequences of revolution is a healthy antidote to the excessive social and economic determinism of some earlier theorists, but it under-plays the very important components of social change and ideological innovation.[31] Nor does it explain the strong egalitarian component in past 'Great Revolutions', including the Bolshevik, with insistent demands for greater participation in decision-making, which is hardly the way to stream-line the state bureaucracy for decisive, modernizing action. One-party dictatorship is a surer way to achieve results than the fumblings of democracy in its infancy.

The last area in which some new theoretical work has been done is in the formulation of hypotheses about the social stages of a 'Great Revolution'. One of the best attacks on this problem was made by Crane Brinton, who was thinking primarily about the French Revolution, but who extended his comparisons to the three other major Western revolutionary movements. He saw the first phase as dominated by moderate bourgeois elements; their supersession by the radicals; a reign of terror; a Thermidorian reaction; and the establishment of strong central authority under military rule to consolidate the limited gains of the revolution. In terms of mass psychology he compared revolution with a fever that rises in intensity, affecting nearly all parts of the body politic, and then dies away.

A much cruder and more elementary model has been advanced by an historian of the revolutions of 1848, Peter Amman.[32] He sees the modern state as an institution holding a monopoly of physical force, administration, and justice over a wide area, a monopoly dependent more on habits of obedience than on powers of coercion. Revolution may therefore be defined as a breakdown of the monopoly due to a failure of these habits of obedience. It begins with the emergence of two or more foci of power, and ends with the elimination of all but one. Amman includes the possibility of 'suspended revolution', with the existence of two or more foci not yet in violent conflict.

This model admittedly avoids some of the difficulties raised by more elaborate classifications of revolution: how to distinguish a *coup d'état* from a revolution; how to define the degrees of social change; how to accommodate the conservative counter-revolution, and so on. It certainly offers some explanation of the progress of revolution from stage to stage as the various power blocks that emerge on the overthrow of the incumbent regime are progressively eliminated; and it explains why the greater the public participation in the revolution, the wider the break with the habits of obedience, and therefore the slower the restoration of order and centralized authority. But it throws the baby out with the bathwater. It is impossible to fit any decentralized traditional society, or any modern federal society, into the model. Moreover, even where it might be applicable, it offers no framework for analysing the roots of revolution, no pointers for identifying the foci of power, no means of distinguishing between the various revolutionary types, and its notion of 'suspended revolution' is little more than verbal evasion.

Though it is set out in a somewhat confused, over-elaborate, and unnecessarily abstract form, the most convincing description of the social stages of revolution is that outlined by Rex D. Hopper.[33] He sees four stages. The first is characterized by indiscriminate, un-co-ordinated mass unrest and dissatisfaction, the result of dim recognition that traditional values no longer satisfy current aspirations. The next stage sees this vague unease beginning to coalesce into organized opposition with defined goals, an important characteristic being a shift of allegiance by the intellectuals from the incumbents to the dissidents, the advancement of an 'evil men' theory, and its abandonment in favour of an 'evil institutions' theory. At this stage there emerge two types of leaders: the prophet, who sketches the shape of the new utopia upon which men's hopes can focus, and the reformer, working methodically toward specific goals. The third, the formal stage, sees the beginning of the revolution proper. Motives and objectives are clarified, organization is built up, a statesman-leader emerges. Then conflicts between the left and the right of the revolutionary movement become acute, and the radicals take over from the moderates. The fourth and last stage sees the legalization of the revolution. It is a product of psychological exhaustion as the reforming drive burns itself out, moral enthusiasm wanes, and economic distress increases. The administrators take over, strong central government is established, and society is reconstructed on lines that embody substantial elements of the old system. The result falls far short of the utopian aspirations of the early leaders, but it succeeds in meshing aspirations with values by partly modifying both, and so allows the reconstruction of a firm social order.

Some of the writing of contemporary social scientists are ingenious feats of verbal juggling in an esoteric language, performed around the totem pole of an abstract model, surrounded as far as the eye can see by the arid wastes of terminological definitions and mathematical formulae. Small wonder the historian finds it hard to digest the gritty diet of this neo-scholasticism, as it has been aptly called. The more historically-minded of the social scientists, however, have a good deal to offer. The history of history, as well as of science, shows that advances depend partly on the accumulation of factual information, but rather more on the formulation of hypotheses that reveal the hidden relationships and common properties of apparently distinct phenomena. For, all their faults, social scientists can supply a corrective to the antiquarian fact-grubbing to which historians are so prone; they can direct attention to problems of general relevance, and away from the sterile triviality of so much historical research; they can ask new questions and suggest new ways of looking at old ones; they can supply new categories, and as a result may suggest new ideas.

Notes

1 Chalmers Johnson, *Revolution and the Social System*, Hoover Institution Studies, 3, Stanford, 1964.

2 Sheldon S. Wolin, 'Violence and the Western political tradition', *American Journal of Orthopsychiatry*, 33, January 1963, pp. 15–28.

3 C. Brinton, *The Anatomy of Revolution*, New York, 1938; L. Gottschalk, 'Causes of revolution', *American Journal of Sociology*, 50, July 1944, pp. 1–8; G. S. Pettee, *The Process of Revolution*, New York, 1938.

4 'Toward a theory of power and political instability in Latin America', *Western Political Quarterly*, 9, 1956. See also D. Bivy, 'Political instability in Latin America: the cross-cultural test of a causal model', *Latin American Research Review*, 3, 1968; W. Dean, 'Latin American Golpes and economic fluctuations, 1823–1966', *Social Science Quarterly*, June 1970.

5 Harry Eckstein, ed., *Internal War*, New York, 1964; 'On the etiology of internal war', *History and Theory*, 4, no 2, 1965, pp. 133–63. I am grateful to Mr Eckstein for allowing me to read this article before publication.

6 The formula has been used – without much success – by an historian, Peter Paret, in *Internal War and Pacification: The Vendée, 1793–96*, Princeton, 1961.

7 Barrington Moore, 'The strategy of the social sciences', in his *Political Power and Social Theory*, Cambridge, Mass., 1958; Ralph Dahrendorf, 'Out of utopia: towards a reorientation of sociological analysis', *American Journal of Sociology*, 64, September 1958, 115–27; C. Wright Mills, *The Sociological Imagination*, New York, 1959; Wilbert E. Moore, *Social Change*, Englewood Cliffs, 1963; T. R. Gurr, *Why Men Rebel*, Princeton, 1970. It should be noted that both the equilibrium and the conflict views of society have very respectable ancestries. The equilibrium model goes back to Rousseau – or perhaps Aquinas; the conflict model to Hobbes, Hegel, and Marx.

8 Quoted in Edward Mead Earle, ed., *Makers of Modern Strategy*, Princeton, 1943, pp. 104–5.

9 *Revolution and the Social System*, Stanford, 1964; a lengthier and modified version of some of these ideas is contained in his *Social Change*, Boston, 1966.

10 N. R. C. Cohn, *Pursuit of the Millennium*, New York, 1961; Eric J. Hobsbawm, *Primitive Rebels*, Manchester, 1959; S. L. Thrupp, 'Millennial Dreams in Action', Supplement 2, *Comparative Studies in Society and History*, The Hague, 1962; A. J. F. Köbben, 'Prophetic movements as an expression of social protest', *Internationales Archiv für Ethnographie*, 49, no. 1, 1960, pp. 117–64.

11 The phrase is not used in his *Social Change*.

12 *Anatomy of Revolution*, op. cit.

13 'On the etiology of internal war', op. cit.

14 P. Amman, 'Revolution: a redefinition', *Political Science Quarterly*, 77, 1962.

15 Emile Durkheim, *Suicide*, The Free Press, Chicago, 1951, pp. 246–54; A. B. Hollingshead, R. Ellis and E. Kirby, 'Social mobility and mental illness', *American Sociological Review*, 19, 1954.

16 M. L. Walzer, 'Puritanism as a revolutionary ideology', *History and Theory*, 3, 1963.

17 T. Parsons, *The Social System*, The Free Press, Chicago, 1951; R. K. Merton, *Social Structure*, The Free Press, Chicago, 1957, ch. 4.

18 W. A. Lewis, 'Commonwealth address', in *Conference Across a Continent*, Toronto, 1963, pp. 46–60; M. Olson, 'Rapid growth as a destabilizing force', *Journal of Economic History*, 23, December 1963, pp. 529. I am grateful to Mr Olson for drawing my attention to Sir Arthur Lewis's article, and for some helpful suggestions.

19 *The Vendée*, Cambridge, Mass., 1964.

20 'Toward a theory of revolution', *American Sociological Review*, 27, February 1962, pp. 1–19, especially the graph on p. 6.

21 W. W. Rostow, *The Stages of Economic Growth*, Cambridge, Mass., 1960; B. Supple, *The Experience of Economic Growth*, New York, 1963, pp. 11–12.

22 E. J. Hobsbawm, 'The crisis of the seventeenth century', in T. H. Aston, ed., *Crisis in Europe, 1560–1660*, London, 1965, pp. 5–58.

23 *La Crise de l'économie française à la fin de l'ancien régime et au début de la révolution*, Paris, 1944.

24 Gabriel Kolko, *Wealth and Power in America*, New York, 1962; Richard M. Titmuss, *Income Distribution and Social Change*, London, 1962.

25 Davies, op. cit., p. 5, quoting Marx, *Selected Works in Two Volumes*, Moscow, 1955, I, p. 947.

26 Daniel Bell, ed., *The Radical Right*, Garden City, 1963.

27 Merton, op. cit., ch. 9.

28 *Why Men Rebel*.

29 G. E. Lenski, 'Status crystallization: a non-vertical dimension of social status', *American Sociological Review*, 19, 1956.

30 C. E. Black, *The Dynamics of Modernization: A Study of Comparative History*, New York, 1966.

31 J. R. Gillis, 'Political decay and the European revolutions, 1789–1848', *World Politics*, 22, 1970.

32 'Revolution: a redefinition', 22, op. cit.

33 'The revolutionary process', *Social Forces*, 28, March 1950, pp. 279–97.

Chapter 2

The social origins of the English Revolution

In the last half-century the historiography of the English Revolution has gone through four fairly well defined stages. First, we had the political narrative, worked out with meticulous care and scholarship by a great Victorian historian, S. R. Gardiner. This religio-constitutional interpretation came under massive attack from the Marxists just before the Second World War, and the comfortable old Whiggish paradigm collapsed to be replaced by a clear-cut conflict between rising bourgeoisie and decaying feudal classes. Next came a short post-war period of dazzling and wildly contradictory theorizing on the basis of the most slender of documentary evidence, until the areas of agreement on every aspect of the problem were reduced to almost zero, and the English Revolution lapsed into the sort of fragmented chaos in which the historiography of the French Revolution wallows today. With both revolutions, once historians have realized that the Marxist interpretation does not work very much better than the Whig, there has followed a period when there is nothing very secure to put in its place. The last twenty years, however, have seen the most remarkable efflorescence of specialized historical monographs, the work of scholars on both sides of the Atlantic who have been prepared to take the infinite pains required for any historical research of enduring value, and who have also had the insight, imagination and intellectual capacity to marshal their findings and to generalize from them. Historians have also adopted more sophisticated models of historical explanation concerning both the nature of early modern society and the feed-back effect upon each other of economics, social structure, ideas, and institutions, to say nothing of the intervention of sheer chance. As a result a good deal of light is at last beginning to penetrate the fog: truth – partial, imperfect, provisional truth – is starting to emerge.

The problem of the social origins of the English Revolution in the seventeenth century was first brought to the attention of historians at large by R. H. Tawney in 1940.[1] He saw a change in the ownership of property occurring in the century before the civil war, by which the old-fashioned landowners decayed and a new class of gentry rose to the top. He attributed this change mainly to differences in the degree of adaptability of estate management to rising prices, to new agricultural techniques and new market outlets, and partly to the presence or absence of non-agricultural sources of wealth. The events of 1640 he interpreted as a shift in the political structure to accommodate the power of the new class of risen gentry. His thesis of social change was supported by two sets of statistics, the one purporting to show a dramatic fall in the manorial holdings of the aristocracy compared with the gentry, and the other a shift in the size of manorial holdings away from the large and towards the medium-sized landowner.

Between 1940 and 1945 English scholars were otherwise engaged, and the issue lay dormant until 1948, when I inadvertently triggered off the controversy by publishing an article on the Elizabethan aristocracy.[2] In this I picked up one element in Tawney's thesis, that of the decline of the aristocracy, pushed it very much further, assigned the cause of decay not to inefficient land management but to over-expenditure, and produced some impressive-looking statistical data, particularly about indebtedness, to support my startling conclusion that 'over two-thirds of the earls and barons were thus swiftly approaching or poised on the brink of financial ruin in the last few years of Queen Elizabeth.' If this ruin was in most cases averted, I attributed it primarily to the largesse of King James.

Three years later this article was subjected to devastating criticism by H. R. Trevor-Roper, who pointed out the extravagance of the language used, the very serious mistakes made in interpreting the statistical evidence for debt, and the unscholarly treatment of much of the ancillary evidence.[3] I replied, withdrawing from my previous exposed position, admitting many errors of statistical interpretation and of fact, but maintaining the general position by the use of some revised statistics of manorial holdings.[4]

Two years later, in 1953, H. R. Trevor-Roper published a full-scale assault on the Tawney thesis itself.[5] So far from seeing the characteristic feature of the age as a rise of the gentry, he postulated instead a massive decline of the 'mere gentry' – small or middling landowners, hard-pressed by inflation and lacking alternative sources of income to maintain their accustomed way of life. Those who rose, according to Trevor-Roper, were, first, the yeomanry, who flourished on the profits of direct farming, rigorous austerity in spending, and systematic saving; and second, those gentry and nobility who had access to the cornucopia of gifts at the disposal of the Crown, or who practised trade or the law. The rising gentry were thus almost exclusively courtiers, court lawyers, and monopoly merchants. The 'mere gentry', who paid for all this largesse, were the 'country party', who in the 1640s overthrew the court system, who fought and defeated the King, and who finally emerged as the radical leaders of the New Model Army, the Independents. Their policy was decentralization, reduction of the costs of litigation, elimination of the detested Court, and destruction of its financial buttresses of state trading and manufacturing monopolies, sale of offices, wards and the like.

The brilliantly formulated argument at first swept all before it. Tawney attempted to defend some of his statistical methods, but he now lacked the vigour to take up the gage of battle which had been thrown down.[6] In 1956 the way seemed to be cleared for general acceptance of the Trevor-Roper thesis, after J. P. Cooper had marshalled a battery of facts and arguments to demonstrate the worthlessness of the statistical methods of both Tawney and myself and had discredited the whole idea that somehow or other the counting of manors could be made to provide a useful indicator of social mobility.[7]

It was not until 1958 and 1959 that the Trevor-Roper thesis in turn came under serious criticism. Both J. E. C. Hill and P. Zagorin pointed out the extreme fragility – indeed, in some cases the non-existence – of certain links in the chain of argument: the equation of 'mere gentry' with small gentry, and small gentry with declining gentry; the assertion that profit could not be made from agriculture in an inflationary era; the assumption that the Court was a smooth highway to riches; the explanation of religious radicalism as a refuge from economic decay; the failure to discuss the Parliamentary leaders of 1642; the identification of the Independents with the 'mere gentry' class; and the description of the policy of the Independents as one of decentralization.[8]

At about the same moment J. H. Hexter published a vigorous attack on both the Tawney and the Trevor-Roper theses;[9] he asserted that Tawney was hypnotized by the Marxist theory of the rise of the bourgeoisie and the decline of feudalism and was trying to fit the events of seventeenth-century England into this pre-determined mould; that Trevor-Roper was obsessed with economic motivation at the expense of ideals and ideology, and saw politics merely as a struggle of the 'Ins' versus the 'Outs', the Court versus the Country, a version of the model set up by Sir Lewis Namier for mid-eighteenth-century England twenty years before. Hexter's own explanation of the social changes prior to 1640 was a new version of my thesis of the decline of the aristocracy. He rejected my concept of financial decay, but argued that there had been a collapse of the military control by the aristocracy over the greater gentry. This meant that political leadership had shifted from the House of Lords to the House of Commons, though the immediate causes of the political breakdown of the 1640s he ascribed to the traditional religious and constitutional factors.

By now it was all too clear that fertility of hypothesis was running far ahead of factual research. What was needed was a massive assault upon the surviving records, economic and personal, of the landed classes of the period, and an examination of the footnotes to the various articles showed that no one had yet done very much work on these lines. Yet as it happened the material had just become available in bewildering profusion. After 1945 the rapid decline of the old land-owning classes caused a flood of private family papers to pour into the newly constituted County Record Offices, where they were catalogued and listed and made available for inspection. As a result the fifteen years 1955–70 saw a crop of doctoral theses upon the finances either of individual families such as the Percys or Hastings, or of a group of well-documented families in certain areas such as Northamptonshire or East Anglia, or of the gentry of a single county such as Yorkshire.[10]

In 1965 I published a book on the aristocracy, based on a lengthy study of private and public archives.[11] In it I developed a new interpretation, an amalgam of some of my earlier ideas and those of J. H. Hexter. I argued that the aristocracy lost military power, territorial possessions and prestige; that their real income declined sharply under Elizabeth, largely due to conspicuous consumption, but recovered equally strongly in the early seventeenth century, largely due to buoyant landed revenues and lavish royal favours. These economic propositions I supported with a good deal of statistical evidence, some of it based on re-formulations of the previously discredited method of counting manors. But in my view, what was important was less the change in relative income than the change in the power and prestige of the magnates relative to that of the greater gentry. I argued that the change left the King and the Church in a dangerously exposed position when they started adopting highly unpopular religious and constitutional policies, and that the débâcle of 1640 was therefore made possible by this prior decline in the power and authority of the peerage.

This hypothesis has been subjected to vigorous criticism, primarily on the grounds that the category of peerage is a poor one for social analysis, since it includes both men whom the French called 'Les Grands', the handful of enormously rich and powerful court families, and also families which in terms of income and style of life were indistinguishable from the topmost levels of the squirarchy. The statistics upon which rests the case for a temporary economic decline have also been seriously questioned.[12] On the other hand the main thesis of a temporary but severe decline of aristocratic prestige and power seems to have survived fairly well. More recently a number of doctoral dissertations on the gentry of particular counties have at last been published, which have been very helpful in eliminating certain hypotheses, and therefore in further narrowing the areas of disagreement. It is hardly possible any longer to regard the declining mere gentry as the backbone of the Revolution,[13] or the Court as an important centre of attraction for the local gentry far from London,[14] or bureaucracy or privateering as the royal road to riches for an aspiring gentleman.[15] More and more the tensions within the society are seen to take the traditional forms of a political conflict between a series of local power élites and the central government, and a religious conflict between Puritans and Anglicans.[16] What has begun to emerge is the social basis for these tensions in the transfer of power and property and prestige to groups of local landed élite, increasingly organized on both a national and a county basis to resist the political, fiscal and religious policies of the Crown; and the parallel shift to new mercantile interests in London, organized to challenge the economic monopoly and political control of the entrenched commercial oligarchy.

It is safe to say that no historical controversy in the last fifty years has attracted so much attention. Why is this? In the first place the area of disagreement appeared to be all-embracing: disagreement over the definition of terms by which to explain the phenomena under discussion; disagreement over what had happened; disagreement over the way it had happened; disagreement over the consequences of what had happened. Such total lack of common ground is very unusual, and its appearance seemed to cast doubt upon the right of the historian to be regarded as an empiricist who bases his enquiries upon reason and proof. Second, the protagonists mustered a prodigious array of talent. The three main contestants,

R. H. Tawney, H. R. Trevor-Roper and J. H. Hexter, are all, in their different ways, very distinguished stylists; they are also that very rare thing, men who are capable of dealing in broad and original conceptual generalizations about the past. Third, the dispute soon developed into a kind of academic gladiatorial show, in which no quarter was offered. There have been few more brutally savage assaults in academic journals than that in which H. R. Trevor-Roper demonstrated the exaggerations and inaccuracies in my first article about the decline of the Elizabethan aristocracy. 'An erring colleague is not an Amalekite to be smitten hip and thigh',[17] protested R. H. Tawney as he nursed his own wounds. Perhaps; but the debate was conducted with a ferocity which not only appealed to the sadism in us all but also gave it a sharp cutting edge.

There were, however, more important grounds for public interest. Many of the younger generation of historians, in France, in England and in the United States, believe that the future of history lies in a cautious selective cross-fertilization with the methods and theories of the social sciences, particularly politics, economics, sociology, social anthropology and social psychology. The problems that arise from any such attempt were brought sharply into focus by the gentry controversy. In the first place it raised, in an acute form, some fundamental problems of methodology. Today every historian, whatever his political persuasion, lays great stress on social forces as operative factors in history. We all talk glibly about social mobility, the rise of the middle classes and so on. This being so, the problem arises of how we are to demonstrate social change in a way that will carry conviction. Social historians of an earlier generation, such as G. M. Trevelyan, constructed their hypotheses on the basis of readily accessible personal documents – the Paston Letters, Pepys's Diary, and so on – bolstered by a certain amount of contemporary comment and by quotations from the imaginative literature of the day from Chaucer to Dickens.[18] These methods were applied, by all parties, to the debate about the gentry. Individual examples of rising peers, decaying peers, rising courtiers, decaying courtiers, rising gentry, decaying gentry were batted triumphantly to and fro. The stream of contemporary comment was quoted extensively, or dismissed as biased and misguided, as the occasion suited. The poets and playwrights were conscripted into the lines of battle. In the hands of dexterous polemicists the result was a bewildering variety of contradictory evidence which to an outside observer above the smoke and noise of conflict seemed to prove precisely nothing at all.

This was a superficial judgment; but what the controversy did bring out more clearly than has ever been apparent before was the shoddy basis of much traditional historical methodology. Plausible rational grounds were found for quite contradictory hypotheses; since the proponent of each theory was free to choose his own evidence, and since there were too many individual facts pointing in too many different ways, this theorizing could not be – and here demonstrably was not being – controlled by facts. This criticism was extended by philosophers to historical methodology as a whole, not without some signs of quiet satisfaction at the humiliation of a sister profession.[19]

It was to meet this objection of the futility of quoting individual examples to demonstrate a sociological proposition that R. H. Tawney attempted to give some scientific basis to his theories by applying the methods of the social sciences: quantitative measurements, systematic sampling and statistical testing. And it is on the reliability or otherwise of the statistical method employed – the counting of manors – that a good deal of the controversy has focused. As a result, a second conclusion of some general significance has emerged; namely, that the use of such methods enormously improves the quality of the evidence, but that in the last resort it is human judgment which determines its reliability: judgment about the meaning of the data, judgment about the way it is handled, judgment about the degree of error involved, judgment about the significance of the conclusions. Though hideous errors have been exposed, though disagreement continues, the whole level of the debate has been raised to a higher plane by the introduction of new, and potentially more empirical, evidence. This part of the debate has pointed the way to a fresh approach to the problems of establishing the direction and measuring the speed of social change in the past; it has also high-lighted the danger of embarking upon statistical calculation without statistical training or advice.

Analogous methodological argument has arisen from the attempts of D. Brunton and D. H. Pennington and of G. Yule to use the mass biographical technique to analyse the composition of the various political groupings in the 1640s.[20] What has become all too clear is that in inexpert or timid hands this tool can become useless or positively misleading. J. E. C. Hill's criticism of the methods of Brunton and Pennington, and D. Underdown's of that of Yule, prove once again that it is necessary to ask the right questions and to employ the right categories if the new techniques of the social sciences are to contribute to the historical discipline more than jargon, obfuscation and a false sense of certainty.[21]

The most serious charge that can be levelled against the protagonists in the debate over the gentry is not so much that they were premature in formulating hypotheses, but that they gave inadequate thought to problems of classification, and that they were unwilling to recognize the large number of questions which had yet to be answered satisfactorily. Like the standard of living of the English worker in the early nineteenth century, or the quality of education in late seventeenth-century Massachusetts, the dispute has thrown up a vast mass of contradictory evidence and disputed statistics. Of the latter controversy Professor Bailyn has written: 'We seem to be dealing here with one of those "questions mal posées" that need restatement before they can be answered.'[22] This is equally true of the gentry controversy, and the search for new definitions of terms and new categories has been in progress for fifteen years or more.

If the historian is to reduce his evidence to intelligible order he is obliged to use abstract concepts and collective nouns. In discussing society he deals in groups labelled peasants, yeomen, gentry and aristocracy; or tenants and landlords, wage-labourers and capitalists; or lower class, middle class and upper class; or Court and Country; or bourgeois and feudal. Some of these categories, like titular aristocracy, are status groups; some, like capitalists, are economic classes with similar incomes derived from similar sources; some like 'Court', describe groups whose income, interests and geographical location are all temporarily based on a single institution. Every individual can be classified in many different ways, and the problem of how to choose the most meaningful categories is particularly difficult when dealing with mobile societies like that of seventeenth-century England. In 1640 do the divisions between titular status groups bear any statistically significant relation to divisions between classes based on differences of wealth, prestige and sources of wealth; has the category of gentlemen been expanded to such a degree as to be valueless for analytical purposes; if so, what is to be put in its place, how is the gentry to be subdivided? It was failure to clarify these issues in the first place which led to so much misunderstanding and recrimination as the debate proceeded. There is, moreover, the danger of treating these abstractions as personalized entities. In assessing the motives of the single individual, the precise admixture of calculation and emotion, the effects of heredity and environment, are difficult enough to determine even when the evidence is available in unusual quantities. How much more complicated it all becomes when it is a question of handling these abstract nouns, of dissecting them and of perceiving the precise relevance of the various threads which make up the pattern not of individual but of collective behaviour.

This is not exclusively a problem that besets the social historian, since it applies equally to the handling of religious or political history in this revolutionary age, for terms like Royalist or Parliamentarian, Presbyterian or Independent, have been shown to be applicable to individuals only with respect to certain issues at certain specific times.[23] To very few men active in public affairs can a single political or religious label be attached which remains valid from, say, 1638 to 1662. This is because the English Revolution, like all others we know of, tended to devour its own children. The alignment of forces of 1640 was quite different from that of 1642, by which time a large block of former Parliamentarians had moved over to reluctant Royalism; it was different again in 1648, when the conservative element among the Parliamentarians, misleadingly known as the Presbyterians, swung back to the side of the King. In 1640 or 1642 virtually no one was republican; in 1649 England was a republic. In 1640 or 1642 virtually no one favoured religious toleration; by 1649 wide toleration for Protestants was achieved. One of the major causes of the muddled thinking about the causes of the English Revolution has arisen from the failure to establish precisely which stage of the Revolution is being discussed. Since each stage was triggered off by different immediate issues, since each was made possible by different long-term movements of society and ideology, and since each was directed by a different section of society, these distinctions are vitally important. It is a measure of the insularity of English historians that they have failed to profit from the lessons to be drawn from studies on the French Revolution, where the need for strict periodization when advancing theories of social causation has been obvious for over a century.

Another methodological difficulty arises from the lamentable fact that a single individual may be classed as gentry, bourgeois, country, capitalist and puritan, each valid for certain analytical purposes, none adequate as a single all-embracing characterization. Under each label, moreover, the individual will find himself lumped together with others, only some of whom will be his companions under other labels, and only a few under all of them. It is this multiple variability of categorization which makes the task of the social historian so extremely difficult.

J. H. Hexter has been particularly active in demonstrating the dangers and confusions which may arise from the use as opposing categories of concepts like middle class and feudal class, gentry and aristocracy, court and country, Presbyterian and Independent.[24] His demolition work is invaluable, but the historian must perforce work with some such collective vocabulary; other words, other concepts have therefore to be invented in their place, or the old ones have to be used with greater sophistication and a greater awareness of their artificiality. As R. H. Tawney observed: 'Categories so general are not useless and cannot be discarded. Apart from their serviceableness as missiles in the mutual bombardment of historians, they have the virtue of suggesting problems, if at times they increase the difficulty of solving them.'

Political ideas are equally liable to misinterpretation, and J. Shklar has brilliantly demonstrated how Harrington has been refashioned generation after generation to suit the preconceptions and preoccupations of the commentators.[25] A more striking example of the subjectivity of scholarship could hardly be found. Similarly, it is necessary to be particularly careful when handling the evidence of contemporaries. For example, Royalists' propaganda, repeated subsequently by Clarendon, was concerned to cast doubts on both the purity of the motives and the social standing of their opponents. They therefore put it about that the Parliamentarians were activated by selfish ambitions for profit and office, and that they were men of inferior status, many of whom gained a living from disreputable trades. It is noticeable that both these ideas (which are part of the stock official line about any group of rebels, from the Pilgrimage of Grace to the Essex Rebellion) are reflected in the Trevor-Roper thesis of a declining 'mere gentry' driven on by a desire to become the 'Ins' rather than the 'Outs'. This hypothesis has striking similarities to the modern assumption of a decaying petit-bourgeois base to Nazism, Fascism and such later manifestations as Poujadism, McCarthyism and Agnewism.

Lastly, there is the question of objectivity. It seems clear that in history, as in the social sciences, the hypothesis of the rigid segregation of facts and values is quite unrealistic. E. H. Carr believes that the first question a student must ask is what are the political and religious beliefs and the social background of the historian he is reading.[26] The validity of this hypothesis is raised obliquely by the widely differing interpretations of the social origins of the Civil War and of the aspirations of the rebel leaders advanced by a conservative anti-clerical like H. R. Trevor-Roper, by a Christian socialist like R. H. Tawney, by a highly sophisticated Marxist like J. E. C. Hill of the late 1950s and 1960s, by an American liberal like J. H. Hexter and by an agnostic English liberal (which is not quite the same thing) like myself. How far has the way we look at the seventeenth century been affected by our political and religious attitudes towards the twentieth?

As well as these questions of methodology, the controversy has also raised important issues of substance, which are of general application over a wide field of historical studies. In one way or another they are all tied up with the question of what causes revolutions. And since it looks as if the twentieth century above all others is going to be the age of revolutions and counter-revolutions, this is a matter of some interest to politicians and planners as well as to historians. In the first place, is it possible to construct a 'model' of a revolutionary situation, or is P. Zagorin correct in arguing that 'there is not, in fact, any model pattern of a bourgeois revolution, and while the investigation of analogies can be most illuminating, there are far more differences between the English and the French Revolutions than analogies'?[27] Assuming that there are uniformities, what sort of a revolution was that of seventeenth-century England? Is it a revolution of a class in full decline, or of a class whose expectations were rising even faster than its objective situation? Is it a protest movement of socially frustrated and economically stagnant or declining mere gentry or of rich and rising gentry temporarily thwarted in their aspirations by the arbitrary taxation, the religious policy and the authoritarian rule of the Eleven Years' Tyranny? On the other side, was there a court group whose ever-increasing size, wealth and arrogance provoked the outsiders to rebellion? Or were Crown, Court, Church and Aristocracy all sinking – either absolutely or relatively – in power, wealth and prestige, and so tempting the outsiders to seize control? Can the two sides of the Civil War really be equated, as the Marxists would have it, with the rising bourgeoisie on the one hand, and the declining feudal classes on the other?

A related problem, first posed in this particular form by H. R.

Trevor-Roper, is whether or not the English revolution is part of a general European movement.[28] The nation state, with its complex bureaucratic structure, its extensive interference in the private lives of its subjects and its huge financial and military resources, is perhaps the most striking, if not the most admirable, contribution of Western civilization to the world over the past five hundred years. It is generally agreed that decisive steps forward in this evolution took place towards the end of the fifteenth century, and that the middle of the seventeenth century saw a major crisis of some sort in most of the great European states: England, France and Spain were all wracked by revolutionary movements on a considerable scale. Are these revolutions similar in character and causation; and, if so, what is it they have in common? H. R. Trevor-Roper believes that they *are* similar, and that their basic characteristic is a revolt of the under-privileged and over-taxed 'country' against the expanding, oppressive, corrupt and authoritarian courts and bureaucracies of the age; that it was in fact the last, futile attempt to stop the process of national centralization before the age of absolutism set in. This thesis has since been developed for England on a large scale by P. Zagorin, but what is still in dispute is whether England possessed a bureaucracy and court on a scale at all comparable to those of Brussels, Paris, or Madrid, and whether the aspirations of the Parliamentary opposition of 1640–2 were in fact anti-Court and decentralizing in character.[29] This raises the question of whether England between the mid-sixteenth and mid-twentieth century should be considered as a normal part of the European scene, or as an idiosyncratic sport best studied in isolation.

Not all historians are agreed that great events must necessarily have great causes. There are those who see the breakdown of 1640 and the war of 1642 as the product merely of a series of political blunders by certain individuals in positions of power.[30] If one takes this view, the whole controversy over the trend of social movement in the previous half-century becomes totally beside the point. The objection to this, however – and to my mind a decisive objection – is that it muddles up two quite different things: the *preconditions*, the long-term social, economic and ideological trends that make revolutions possible, and which are subject to comparative analysis and generalization; and the *triggers*, the personal decisions and the accidental pattern of events which may or may nor set off the revolutionary outbreak, and which are unique and unclassifiable.

Finally there are serious differences of opinion about three propositions put forward by Karl Marx (indeed, at one stage the discussion threatened to get mixed up with the battle of Cold War ideologies). One theory, first advanced by Aristotle, revived by Harrington in the seventeenth century and reformulated by Marx in the nineteenth, is that a constitution is a direct reflection of the distribution of social and economic power; consequently, the two must alter in step together if major upheavals are to be avoided. The main weakness of Harrington's doctrine, and the aspect which distinguishes it most sharply from that of Marx, is his obsessive preoccupation with landed property to the exclusion of all other forms of wealth. But this was not altogether unrealistic in the seventeenth-century English context, despite the growing resources and political influence of the London mercantile and financial community. This view, moreover, was not merely confined to a handful of members of the Rota Club, as H. R. Trevor-Roper has suggested.[31] The prolonged parliamentary debate on the revival of a second chamber in 1659 shows that there was considerable agreement in the House of Commons on the Harringtonian thesis of the relationship of the constitution to the balance of property, though only the Republicans thought – wrongly as it turned out – that the peers had lost most of their property and that the balance had consequently been destroyed rather than modified.

We can see today that this hypothesis needs to be qualified in various ways, and in particular that very much greater weight needs to be given to ideological enthusiasm, military force and traditional habits of obedience, which together or in isolation may often outweigh crude economic pressures. Like Hobbes, Harrington had little understanding of the complex web of social relationships which bind man to man, quite apart from the economic and physical necessity for co-operation and obedience. He failed altogether to recognize the force of passion and prejudice, even though his own political theories and actions were in large measure dictated by an impractical admiration for the Roman Republic. He did realize that in certain cases, such as the Norman Conquest of England or the Spanish Conquest of Central America, violence has been used to redistribute wealth and power in a manner appropriate to the new – and extremely tenacious – political establishment. More frequently, political power has been manipulated to channel wealth into the hands of the ruling élite, thus keeping the social structure and the political constitution in line by adjusting the former to the latter, rather than vice versa. It was Sir Thomas More who produced the disillusioned judgment:[32]

> when I consider and weigh in my mind all these commonwealths, which nowadays anywhere do flourish, so God help me I can perceive nothing but a certain conspiracy of rich men procuring their own commodities under the name and title of the commonwealth. They invent and devise all means and crafts, first how to keep safely, without fear of losing, that they have unjustly gathered together, and next how to hire and abuse the work and labour of the poor for as little money as may be. These devices, when the rich men have decreed to be kept and observed under colour of the commonality, that is to say, also of the poor people, then they be made laws.

With these important qualifications – with some of which Harrington is not altogether in disagreement – the view that there must be a direct relationship between social structure and political institutions and that the former tends to dictate the latter, is widely accepted today, even by historians and politicians of a strongly anti-Marxist cast of mind. It is generally agreed, for example, that land reform is a necessary preliminary to the introduction of democratic institutions and ideals in Latin America.

The notion that constitutional or administrative history can be studied in a social vacuum, as an isolated story of the growth of liberty or bureaucracy or whatever, is one that few historians are now prepared to countenance. The problems of power and its distribution are seen to be entangled with the whole complex of nurture, education and the family system, social norms and ethical values, religious beliefs and ecclesiastical organization, the land law, status hierarchy and economic structure of the society as a whole. The major problem is to explain how, and to what extent, the various parts all fit together.

The second of Marx's theories is that the first major shift in European society was from the feudal to the bourgeois phase, which occurred in the seventeenth century in England and in the late eighteenth century in France. It was Engels who produced the first full-blown explanation of how the English Revolution fitted into the Marxist interpretative framework. He achieved this by some brisk legerdemain which changed nobles and gentry into 'bourgeois landlords', and thus made it possible to regard the Revolution as a 'bourgeois upheaval'. The end result was the creation of a state based on the compromise of 1689, by which 'The political spoils of "pelf and place" were left to the great landowning families, provided that the enormous interests of the financial, manufacturing and commercial middle class was sufficiently attended to.'[33] This theory of Engels lies at the back of Tawney's definition of the rising gentry as progressive-minded and capitalist and of the Royalist supporters as old-fashioned and feudal. It was not until the 1950s that this old equation of the gentry with the bourgeoisie was severely criticized by J. H. Hexter and P. Zagorin, on both logical and factual grounds.[34]

The third proposition of Marx which is involved in the controversy concerns the relationship of social and economic forces on the one hand, and ideology on the other. Marx tended to see the latter as a sociologically motivated superstructure and H. R. Trevor-Roper similarly seems to regard religion as economically determined.[35] Tawney took a far more sophisticated view of the relationship between ideas and interests, but his interpretation also laid great stress on material motives. It is doubtful whether he was prepared to give much weight to the ostensible issues of political liberty and religious reform in assessing the causes of the upheavals of the 1640s. Hill has moved from an assumption that ideas are largely mere superstructure to a position where they loom larger and larger as historical forces in their own right.[36] So complex is the human personality that materialism and idealism, reason and emotion, interests and morals, are constantly confused, first one and then the other rising to the surface. There is no final solution to this problem, and every historian must work according to his private judgment. At bottom it seems to come down to whether he takes an optimistic or a pessimistic view of human nature: optimists stress ideals, pessimists material interests.

Looking back on the controversy today, it seems clear that all parties in the early stages were taking an indefensibly narrow view of the causes of revolution. They paid too much attention to changes in the distribution of wealth, and too little to less tangible factors, such as changing ideals, aspirations and habits of obedience. They confused two different things: a material and moral weakening of the ruling élite, and a strengthening of the size and intensity of the dissident elements. Above all they failed to see that revolutions have extremely complicated origins, and that social causes are only one among many. What can be said in defence of the protagonists, however, is that it is in no small part because of their pioneer efforts and blunders that a more sophisticated view of the causes of the English Revolution is beginning to emerge.

Notes

1 R. H. Tawney, 'Harrington's interpretation of his age', *Proceedings of the British Academy*, 27, 1941.
R. H. Tawney, 'The rise of the gentry, 1558–1640', *Economic History Review*, 11, 1941.

2 L. Stone, 'The anatomy of the Elizabethan aristocracy', *Economic History Review*, 18, 1948.

3 H. R. Trevor-Roper, 'The Elizabethan aristocracy: an anatomy anatomised', *Economic History Review*, 2nd ser., 3, 1951.

4 L. Stone, 'The Elizabethan aristocracy: a restatement', *Economic History Review*, 2nd ser., 4, 1952.

5 H. R. Trevor-Roper, 'The gentry, 1540–1640', *Economic History Review*, Supplement 1, 1953.

6 R. H. Tawney, 'The rise of the gentry: a postscript', *Economic History Review*, 2nd ser., 7, 1954.

7 J. P. Cooper, 'The counting of manors', *Economic History Review*, 2nd ser., 8, 1956.

8 C. Hill, 'Recent interpretations of the Civil War', in *Puritanism and Revolution*, London, 1958.
P. Zagorin, 'The social interpretations of the English Revolution', *Journal of Economic History*, 19, 1959.

9 J. H. Hexter, *Reappraisals in History*, London, 1961.

10 G. R. Batho, 'The finances of an Elizabethan nobleman: Henry Percy, 9th Earl of Northumberland', *Economic History Review*, 2nd ser., 9, 1957.
G. R. Batho, 'The household papers of Henry Percy, 9th Earl of Northumberland', *Camden Society*, 3rd ser., 93, 1962.
C. Cross, *The Puritan Earl, 1536–1595*, London, 1966.
M. E. Finch, *The Wealth of Five Northamptonshire Families, 1540–1640, Northants Record Society Publications*, 19, 1955.
A. Simpson, *The Wealth of the Gentry, 1540–1660*, Chicago, 1961.
J. T. Cliffe, *The Yorkshire Gentry from the Reformation to the Civil War*, London, 1969.

11 L. Stone, *The Crisis of the Aristocracy, 1558–1641*, Oxford, 1965.

12 D. C. Coleman, 'The gentry controversy and the aristocracy in crisis, 1558–1641', *History*, 51, 1966.
J. H. Hexter, 'The English aristocracy, its crisis, and the English Revolution', *Journal of British Studies*, 8, 1968.
E. L. Petersen, 'The Elizabethan aristocracy anatomized, atomized and reassessed', *Scandinavian Economic History Review*, 16, 1968.

13 J. T. Cliffe, op. cit., p. 351.
W. G. Hoskins, 'The estates of the Caroline gentry', in *Devonshire Studies*, ed. W. G. Hoskins and H. P. R. Finberg, London, 1952.

14 J. T. Cliffe, op. cit., p. 85.
W. T. MacCaffrey, 'Place and patronage in Elizabethan politics', in *Elizabethan Government and Society*, ed. S. T. Bindoff *et al.*, London, 1961.
G. E. Aylmer, 'Office-holding as a factor in English history, 1625–42', *History*, 44, 1959.

15 G. Aylmer, op. cit.
L. Stone, 'Office under Queen Elizabeth: the case of Lord Hunsdon and the lord chamberlainship in 1585', *Historical Journal*, 10, 1967; P. Zagorin, 'Sir Edward Stanhope's advice to Thomas Wentworth, Viscount Wentworth, concerning the deputyship of Ireland', *Historical Journal*, 7, 1964.
A. Andrews, *Elizabethan Privateering*, Cambridge, 1964.

16 T. G. Barnes, *Somerset, 1625–1640*, Cambridge, Mass., 1961.
J. T. Cliffe, op. cit., chs 12, 13.
A. Everitt, *Suffolk and the Great Rebellion, 1640–1660, Suffolk Records Society*, 3, 1960.
A. Everitt, *The Community of Kent and the Great Rebellion*, Leicester, 1966.
A. Everitt, *Change in the Provinces: the Seventeenth Century*, Leicester, 1969.

17 R. H. Tawney, op. cit., 1954, p. 97.

18 G. M. Trevelyan, *English Social History*, London, 1942.

19 P. Gardiner, *The Nature of Historical Explanation*, Oxford, 1952.
W. H. Walsh, *An Introduction to the Philosophy of History*, New York, 1960.

20 D. Brunton and D. H. Pennington, *Members of the Long Parliament*, London, 1954.
G. Yule, *The Independents in the English Civil War*, Cambridge, 1958.

21 C. Hill, *Society and Puritanism in Pre-Revolutionary England*, London, 1964.
D. Underdown, 'The Independents reconsidered', *Journal of British Studies*, 3, 1964; See also G. Yule, 'Independents and

Revolutionaries', loc. cit., 7, 1968, and D. Underdown, 'Independents again', loc. cit., 8, 1968.

22 B. Bailyn, *Education in the Forming of American Society*, New York [n.d.], p. 80.

23 J. H. Hexter, 'The Presbyterian Independents', *Reappraisals in History*, London, 1961.
G. E. Aylmer, *The King's Servants: The Civil Service of Charles I, 1625–42*, London, 1961, p. 393; V. Pearl, 'The "Royal Independents" in the English Civil War', *Transactions of the Royal Historical Society*, 5th ser., 18, 1968.

24 J. H. Hexter, op. cit., chs 5, 6, 7.

25 J. Shklar, 'Ideology hunting: the case of James Harrington', *American Political Science Review*, 53, 1959.

26 E. H. Carr, *What is History?*, London, 1962, p. 48.

27 P. Zagorin, 'The social interpretations of the English Revolution', *Journal of Economic History*, 19, 1959, pp. 389–90.

28 H. R. Trevor-Roper, 'The general crisis of the seventeenth century', *Past and Present*, 16, 1959; 18, 1960.

29 P. Zagorin, *The Court and the Country*, London, 1969.

30 C. V. Wedgwood, *The King's Peace, 1637–41*, London, 1955.

31 H. R. Trevor-Roper, 'The gentry, 1540–1640', p. 46.

32 T. More. *Utopia* (Everyman edition), London, p. 112.

33 F. Engels, Introduction to the English Edition of *Socialism: Utopian and Scientific*, London, 1892; reprinted in Marx and Engels, *Basic Writings on Politics and Philosophy*, ed. L. S. Feuer, New York, 1959, p. 57.

34 J. H. Hexter, op. cit., ch. 5.
P. Zagorin, op. cit., pp. 381–87.

35 H. R. Trevor-Roper, op. cit., p. 31.

36 The shift can be traced through: J. E. C. Hill, *The English Revolution*, London, 1940; *The Economic Problems of the Church*, Oxford, 1956; 'La Révolution anglaise du XVIIe siècle (Essai d' interprétation), *Revue Historique*, 221, 1959; *The Century of Revolution, 1603–1714*, Edinburgh, 1961. In a recent statement of his position, he perceptively describes ideas as the steam of history: 'Steam is essential to the driving of a railroad engine; but neither a locomotive nor a permanent way can be built out of steam.' (C. Hill, *Intellectual Origins of the English Revolution*, Oxford, 1965, p. 3.)

Part II

Interpretation

Chapter 3

The causes of the English Revolution

1. Presuppositions

Before advancing an explanation for a historical event, it is first necessary to establish what kind of event it is which needs explaining. What happened in England in the middle of the seventeenth century? Was it a 'Great Rebellion' as Clarendon believed, the last and most violent of the many rebellions against particularly unprepossessing or unpopular kings that had been staged by dissident members of the landed classes century after century throughout the middle ages?[1] Was it merely an internal war caused by a temporary political breakdown due to particular political circumstances? Such is the view of Miss C. V. Wedgwood, who is content to begin her history of the English Civil War in 1637, three years before the collapse of the government, and five years before the outbreak of armed violence.[2] Was it the Puritan revolution of S. R. Gardiner, to whom the driving force behind the whole episode was a conflict of religious institutions and ideologies?[3] Was it the first great clash of liberty against royal tyranny, as seen by Macaulay, the first blow for the Enlightenment and Whiggery, a blow which put England on the slow road to Parliamentary monarchy and civil liberties?[4] Was it the first bourgeois revolution, in which the progressive and dynamic elements in society struggled to emerge from their feudal swaddling clothes? This is how Engels saw it, and how many historians of the 1930s, including R. H. Tawney, and C. Hill, tended to regard it.[5] Was it the first revolution of modernization, which is the Marxist interpretation in a new guise, now perceived as a struggle to remould the institutions of government to meet the needs of a more efficient, more rationalist, and more economically advanced society?[6] Or was it a revolution of despair, engineered by the decaying and backward-looking elements in society, the mere gentry of H. R. Trevor-Roper, who, consumed with hatred, jealousy, and ideological intolerance bred of sectarian religious radicalism, attempted to turn back the clock, and to re-create the decentralized, rural, agrarian, inward-looking, socially stable and economically stagnant society of their hopeless, anachronistic dreams?[7] There is a grain of truth in each of these theories. Each author displays one facet of a many-sided whole, but tends to ignore the sides which do not fit his stereotype, and chooses to focus too exclusively on that particular stage of a many-staged process which best illustrates his particular hypothesis.

In order to clear the way for the long-term analysis which will follow, it is first necessary to set out certain basic presuppositions upon whose acceptance the whole structure depends. The first and most fundamental is that there is a profound truth in James Harrington's assertion that 'the dissolution of this Government caused the War, not the War the dissolution of this Government.'[8] This means that to concentrate upon Clarendon's 'Great Rebellion' or Miss Wedgwood's 'Civil War' is to miss the essential problem. The outbreak of war itself is relatively easy to explain; what is hard is to puzzle out why most of the established institutions of State and Church – Crown, Court, central administration, army, and episcopacy – collapsed so ignominiously two years before.

The second assumption is that this is more than a mere rebellion against a particular king. Sigmund Neumann has defined a revolution as involving 'a sweeping, fundamental change in political organization, social structure, economic property control, and the predominant myth of a social order, thus indicating a major break in the continuity of development'.[9] If we accept this definition, it is evident that the English Revolution fulfils some, but not all, of these requirements. There was undoubtedly for a time a fundamental change in political organization, and in the predominant myth of a social order, and the Levellers certainly demanded a fundamental change in social structure, although admittedly they were soon crushed. On the other hand, much (but not all) of the old political organization was restored in 1660, and although economic property control was (temporarily) seized from the hands of the crown and the episcopacy, both Independents and Presbyterians were satisfied with the existing distribution of private property within society. They were also determined to retain the existing hierarchy of ranks and its close association with the pattern of authority. Even Cromwell, who took the lead in abolishing monarchy, the House of Lords and episcopacy, was in the end a conservative in social matters. By 1654 he knew where he stood, and spoke approvingly of 'the ranks and orders of men, whereby England hath been known for hundreds of years: a nobleman, a gentleman, a yeoman; the distinction of these. That is a good interest of the nation and a great one. The natural magistracy of the nation, was it not trampled under foot ... by men of Levelling principle?'[10]

Such attempts to change the distribution of property as were made, notably by the confiscation and sale of the estates of important Royalists, are now known to have been largely unsuccessful, and in terms of the spread of wealth between social groups, and even between individual families, England at the end of the revolution in 1660 was barely distinguishable from England at the beginning in 1640.[11] Within these limits, however, the English Revolution is none the less unique among the many rebellions of early modern Europe for its political and religious radicalism and cannot easily be compared with the colonial revolts of Ireland, the Netherlands, Catalonia, or Portugal, with the aristocratic and official revolt of the Fronde, or with any of those desperate, blind, and bloody movements of popular fury by peasantry or urban poor which tore at seventeenth-century Europe from Calais to the Urals.

The revolutionary nature of the English Revolution can be demonstrated partly by its deeds and partly by its words. Its achievements included not merely the killing of a king (the English had a long tradition of murdering unwanted kings, from William Rufus to Edward II to Richard II), but the putting of a king on trial in the name of 'the people of England', on a charge of high treason for violation of 'the fundamental constitutions of this Kingdom'.[12] This was something which had never been done before. The Revolution involved not merely the substitution of one king for another but the abolition of the institution of monarchy; not merely the execution of the persons and the confiscation of the property of a few noblemen, but the abolition of the House of Lords; not merely a protest against Hobbes's 'unpleasing priests', clergy and bishops, but the sweeping away of the Established Church and the seizure of episcopal properties; not merely an attack on unpopular officials, but the abolition of a range of critically important administrative and legal institutions of government. The revolutionary nature of the English Revolution is perhaps even more convincingly demonstrated by its words than by its deeds. The mere fact that it was such an extraordinarily wordy revolution — well over 22,000 sermons, speeches, pamphlets and newspapers were published between 1640 and 1661[13] — would by itself strongly suggest that this is something very different from the familiar protest against an unpopular government. This torrent of printed words is evidence of a clash of ideas and of ideologies, and the emergence of radical concepts affecting every aspect of human behaviour and every institution in society from the family to the Church to the State.

Some have argued that because much of the rhetoric, particularly in the early stages, was couched in terms of a return to some imagined golden age in the past, because the word 'revolution' itself normally meant not a change to something totally new, but a circular or elliptical rotation to a position which had been occupied at some earlier moment in time, therefore the movement was basically conservative, and consequently not a revolution at all as the word is defined today. Now it is perfectly true that reformers and reactionaries in 1640 were each looking back to a (different) mythical past. The Puritans, of whatever persuasion, were seeking a return to what they imagined to have been the state of the primitive Christian Church of the Early Fathers, before it had been distorted and corrupted by later, sinful, accretions. Radical conservatives like William Prynne, who wanted a cultural counter-revolution to change morality and life styles, to abolish long hair, stage plays and fornication from the land, based their beliefs on a theory of the falling away of the race from its pristine purity: 'Strange it is and lamentable to consider, how far our nation is of late degenerated from what it was in former ages.'[14] The lawyers were seeking to go back to what they believed to be the medieval situation – and were they not assured by Chief Justice Sir Edward Coke in immensely learned folio volumes that it was no more than the historical truth? – when kings, bureaucracies, and church courts were all guided and controlled by the opinions of common lawyers and the conventions of the common law.[15] The antiquarians provided the more advanced lawyers and parliamentarians with the theory of the Norman Yoke, the notion that before 1066 the Anglo-Saxons had lived as free and equal citizens, enjoying self-government through representative institutions, but that these liberties had been destroyed by an alien tyranny of kings and aristocrats imposed by the Norman Conquest.[16] Somewhat imprudently exploited by the landed opposition to the Crown in the 1620s and the early 1640s, this theory of the Norman Yoke was taken up by the Levellers in the late 1640s as a weapon against landlords as a whole. Meanwhile the parliamentary gentry were dreaming of a golden age of political harmony between Crown and Parliament and a Protestant domestic and foreign policy, which they believed to have existed in the good old days of Queen Elizabeth and to which they hoped to return.

Charles I and his authoritarian supporters similarly looked back to the reigns of rich and strong kings like Henry II, Edward I, or Henry VIII, when the powers of the executive were at their maximum. Laud cast envious eyes back to the vastly wealthy, politically powerful and socially well-connected church of the late middle ages, while Charles himself and some of his advisers had visions of restoring an antediluvian past when social hierarchy was respected, deference reigned supreme, social mobility was at a minimum, and every man knew his place. The fact that these notions were cast in an antiquarian mould does nothing to alter one way or another the degree of radicalism or conservatism which they represent. This must be judged against the contemporary situation, and it makes no difference whatever whether the idealized golden age is in the past or in the future. As Hobbes observed, 'No man can have in his mind a conception of the future, for the future is not yet. But of our conceptions of the past, we make a future.'[17] What matters, therefore, is the degree to which the reality of the present differs from the image of the past, and the degree of determination to override all obstacles in order to make the one conform to the other.

It is perfectly true that the country gentry and nobility assembled in Westminster in 1640 were reformers, not revolutionaries. They had no intention whatever of tampering with the social structure, and although they wished to make far-reaching changes in the essential organs of Church and State, they stopped far short of any plans for the overthrow of established institutions. In 1640 no one dreamed of abolishing the monarchy or the House of Lords, and only a minority hoped to abolish episcopacy or tithes. Notions of participatory democracy were beginning to circulate among the more radical Puritan congregations, but none of the élite saw this as anything more than a small cloud on the distant horizon.

On the other hand, even if the Parliamentary opposition leaders were political and religious moderates and were undeniably social conservatives, and even if most of their arguments were legalistic and backward-looking, it should not be forgotten that as early as 1640 many of them were using, and complacently listening to, language which was genuinely and frankly radical in both tone and content.[18] Even so cautious a man as Sir Edward Hyde, the future Royalist leader, was caught up in the euphoria of the moment and was to be heard talking about 'a dawning of a fair and lasting day of happiness to this kingdom'. In November 1641 Sir John Dryden of

Canons Ashby, M.P., a highly respectable, wealthy and well-established Northamptonshire gentleman, wrote from London to his uncle in the country to describe the activities of the Long Parliament:

> I ask that I shall have your prayers . . . I can only bring
> straw and stubble to that great work. God be praised, here
> want not skillful agents for that great work; it hitherto
> goeth on fast . . . The walls go up fast, though they cannot
> be suddenly finished. The ruins be such, both in Church
> and Commonwealth, that some years will hardly repair
> all the breaches.

Ostensibly, Sir John is speaking of putting things back to order, of repairing decay, of going back to something which existed before, but so different was the reality of the present from his vision of the past and the future, and so heavy in mystical overtones was his language, that it is reasonable to doubt the moderation of his ambitions. Proof of this contention is provided by the more millenarian tone adopted by many of the laity. In 1641 Samuel Hartlib, who was patronized by Pym, was talking hopefully about 'the reformation of the whole world', and expressing his confidence that Parliament would 'lay the cornerstone to the world's happiness'. In the summer of 1642 a Yorkshire gentleman wrote to an M.P. expressing his 'hearty desires for a thorough reformation both of Church and Commonwealth', and assuring his friend of his confidence that Parliament was 'able if need require to build a new world'.[19]

If M.P.s and their friends were using Utopian language among themselves, some of the rhetoric to which they were exposed was even more extravagant. In 1641 Jeremy Burroughs gave the assembled members of the House of Commons a sermon entitled 'Zion's Joy', in which he spoke ecstatically of 'a very jubilee and resurrection of Church and State', while Thomas Case called them in apocalyptic language to the exercise of even greater zeal in the cause of change:[20]

> Reformation must be universal . . . Reform all places, all
> persons and callings. Reform the benches of judgment, the
> inferior magistrates . . . Reform the universities, reform the
> cities, reform the counties, reform inferior schools of learning.
> Reform the Sabbath, reform the ordinances, the worship of
> God . . . You have more work to do than I can speak . . .

Every plant which my heavenly Father hath not planted
shall be rooted up.

This is not the language of aristocratic rebellion or civil war, with
limited, largely personal, objectives; it is the language of revolution
in the modern sense, and the language of 'cultural revolution' at
that. And yet it was preached in 1641, before the war began, to an
approving audience of sober-sided members of Parliament – although
admittedly an audience whose susceptibility had been artificially
heightened by the physical deprivations of a fast. Meanwhile in the
streets and taverns public opinion was being aroused by a spate of
pamphlet literature that brought the fundamental issue of authority
directly to a large and eager public. As a result, Hobbes described
the kingdom in the years before the war as 'boiling hot with questions
concerning the right of dominion and the obedience due from
subjects'. Indeed Henry Parker had already formulated for the
benefit of the Parliamentarians a theory of sovereignty according to
which the source of political power lay in the common consent and
agreement of all subjects, Parliament was supreme by virtue of
representing the whole community, and the subjects reserved the
ultimate right of resistance against the arbitrary exercise of executive
power.[21] Here was novelty indeed, ideas that were to produce strange
fruits before the decade was out.

Indeed ten years later the Parliamentary leaders were talking
excitedly of exporting political revolution all over Europe, using
language and tactics which have a familiar ring in the twentieth
century. In 1651, on the occasion of a vist by the English fleet to
Cadiz, Admiral Blake caused justifiable irritation to King Philip IV
by announcing to his host:[22]

in the public square there, that, with the example afforded
by London, all Kingdoms will annihilate tyranny and become
republics. England had done so already; France was following
in her wake; and as the natural gravity of Spaniards rendered
them somewhat slower in their operations, he gave them ten
years for the revolution in their country.

In the light of this sort of language, used not by radical fringe groups
but by prominent members of the regime, it is a little hard to understand those historians who would deny the word revolution to what
happened in mid-seventeenth-century England.

From all this one may reasonably conclude that by the time the government collapsed in 1640 there existed among very large numbers of normally conservative noblemen and gentlemen a strong desire for widespread change, a change in the political myth away from the Divine Right of Kings, a change in the constitution away from an all-powerful executive and towards a 'balanced constitution' in which authority would be distributed more evenly between the king and his servants and the representative assembly of the political nation; a change in legal and administrative arrangements, with the destruction of most of the so called 'prerogative courts'; a change in the powers, wealth and organization of the Established national Church; and finally a modest but strictly limited change in the concept of social hierarchy, by which gentlemen would be treated more or less as equals, regardless of discrepancies in titular rank.

The third assumption upon which this essay is founded is that the class war theory of the Marxists has only limited applicability to the seventeenth century. The great contribution of Marxism to the interpretation of the period has been to stress the extent and significance of early capitalist growth in trade, industry and agriculture in the century before the revolution. Marxist or Marxist-influenced historians have taken the lead in investigating these developments and it is important to recognize how much their work has affected all subsequent interpretations. Their weakness, however, has been their persistent efforts to link these developments to the revolution by means of a theory of class warfare that may work reasonably well for England in the early nineteenth century, but which seriously distorts the social reality of earlier periods. A more fruitful way of linking social and economic change to revolution is through the theory of status inconsistency, which holds that a society with a relatively large proportion of persons undergoing high mobility is likely to be in an unstable condition.[23]

The revolution was certainly not a war of the poor against the rich, for one of its most striking features was the almost total passivity of the rural masses, the copyholders and agricultural labourers. In contrast to the peasant risings during the French or Russian Revolutions (or indeed in France or Russia in the seventeenth century), the rural poor in England were almost entirely neutral during the 1640s and 1650s. In 1640–2 a number of enclosures were torn down by rioting peasantry acting on the not unreasonable assumption that with the partial collapse of government 'they will take advantage of these times, lest they have not the like again.'[24]

In the late 1640s the Diggers made a few pathetic and easily crushed attempts to take over the common lands here and there; but that was all. The only serious interventions by the rural poor in the whole course of the revolution were the assemblies of 'clubmen' who gathered in several counties during the latter stages of the war.[25] These were no more than desperate attempts by the rural poor to protect their fields, crops, cattle and women from the depredations of both armies, and themselves from the clutches of the recruiting officers of both sides. Indeed, evidence of the lack of enthusiasm of the poor for the war is provided by the fact that both sides were so soon obliged to resort to conscription to fill the ranks of the modest armies which were all they could afford.

The wage-earners in the towns were equally passive, even in London. On the other hand there can be no doubt that one stage up the social ladder, among the small freeholders and yeomen in the countryside, and among the apprentices, artisans and small shop-keepers in the towns, there was a definite tendency to side with Parliament. But the rich merchant oligarchies in the cities were either cautiously and selfishly neutral or sided with the King as the protector and patron of their political and economic privileges. The only exceptions to this rule were when religious convictions or resentment at previous ill-treatment triumphed over the calcula-tions of interest. The bourgeoisie, therefore, was either neutral or divided. Moreover, the fissure did not run along lines of class, of employer against employee, but rather along lines of relative wealth and access to political and economic privilege.

The gentry were equally neutral or divided, without any clearly marked division on lines of wealth. There were plenty of rich gentry who were active Parliamentarians, especially in the early stages, and an analysis of the political affiliations of the richer gentry M.P.s in the Long Parliament reveals an almost even split on either side.[26] Nor can the poorer parish gentry legitimately be identified with either side. With the radicalization of the parliamentary party in the middle and late 1640s under the pressure of a long-drawn and inconclusive war, a minority of small gentry thrust themselves to the fore, both in the local county committees and in national politics. Many, perhaps a majority, of the 'Political Independents' were of small gentry origin. But this does not mean that the 'mere gentry' can be described as Parliamentarian. In the north and west these little men, these archetypal mere gentry, formed the backbone of the Royalist army and party in the 1640s, and were to be the most fanatical of Church and King men in the post-revolution era. Equally damaging to the hypothesis of the 'mere gentry' as predominantly Parliamentarian is the discovery that the mere gentry of Kent formed the core of the Royalist opposition as well as the core of the Parliamentary County Committee.[27] In short, the fact that many members of the radical group which seized control of the Parliamentary forces in the late 1640s were lesser gentry does not at all mean that the lesser gentry as a whole were mostly Parliamentarian. There is a logical fallacy in this chain of reasoning which is too obvious to be worth dwelling upon any further.[28]

A more promising argument about the division of the gentry in the revolution is that the money-minded, enterprising, entrepreneurial (i.e. bourgeois) gentry tended to side with Parliament, and the paternalistic, conservative, rentier (i.e. feudal) gentry tended to side with the King.[29] This is an attractive notion, but there is at present not a shred of evidence to support it. It is certainly a fact that the south and east were mostly in the hands of the Parliamentarians and the north and west in the hands of the Royalists. But to shift from this geographical division to the identification of individual characteristics in the two areas is to fall into the well-known ecological fallacy.[30] It is possible to think of a number of reasons – nearer or farther distance from London, stronger or weaker Puritan leanings, greater or lesser exposure to initial seizure by Parliamentary forces from London when the war began, etc. – why the geographical split should have occurred the way it did, without concluding that it necessarily represents a bourgeois-feudal dichotomy.

To sum up, therefore, the only sociological conclusions which seem plausible for the early stages of the war are that there was a clearly marked tendency 'for the yeomen in the countryside and middling groups in the towns and industrial areas to side with Parliament, and a much less marked tendency for the aristocracy and the merchant oligarchies to side with the King. None of the polarities of feudal-bourgeois, employer-employee, rich-poor, rising-declining, county-parish gentry seem to have much relevance to what actually happened in the early 1640s. What we have to explain is a complex struggle of orders and status groups, largely confined to members of various élites which were fissured and fragmented by differences about constitutional arrangements, religious aspirations and cultural patterns, by conflicts of interest and conflicts of loyalty, as well as by the unsettling effects of rapid economic development and social change. Before civil war could break out, it was necessary for the major institutions of central government to lose their credibility and to collapse. Although the crisis only becomes intelligible in the light of social and economic change, what has to be explained in the first place is not a crisis within the society, but rather a crisis within the regime, the alienation of very large segments of the élites from the established political and religious institutions. The first stage of the crisis was a conflict within the élites rather than a challenge to the existing social order. This was a political revolution with potential, but abortive, social consequences, whereas the French Revolution was a political revolution with partially realized social consequences. As the Levellers bluntly put it to the House of Commons in 1647, 'the ground of the late war between the King and you was a contention whether he or you should exercise the supreme power over us.'[31] In other words, the war began as a power struggle between competing elements of the pre-existing structure of authority.

Any analysis of so complex a thing as a revolutionary challenge to an established regime, even one mounted largely from within the ruling élites, must necessarily range backwards over a long period of time and be multi-causal in its approach, laying as much stress on institutional defects and ideological passions as on social movements and economic changes, if it is to have any hope of grasping all the threads that lead to the crisis. Such an approach raises serious problems of organization, and for analytical purposes it seems best to unravel the tangled skein of the developing crisis stage by stage, examining first the long-term preconditions, next the medium-term precipitants, and lastly the short-term triggers. Such an organization of the material does not imply that the seamless web of history tears neatly apart into hard and fast categories of this kind, for it clearly does nothing of the sort. All that is claimed is that this seems the most appropriate way of arranging the mass of material into an easily intelligible and logically consequential order. Moreover, an attempt such as this to set down an enormously complicated train of events in relatively short compass inevitably involves some degree of over-simplification and over-assertive dogmatism. If the reader is to follow the thread of the argument without getting lost, the qualifications, the shades of meaning and the ambiguities must not be overstressed. The multi-causal approach provides a much closer approximation to the infinite complexity of real life than either an apparently straightforward narrative, or an explanation which hinges around a single determining cause.

The problem remains, however, of how to arrange the causes enumerated in a rank order of relative importance. If no such ordering is attempted, the reader is left with an unweighted bundle of causes, but he must recognize that in the last resort the imposition of a rank ordering depends not on objective and testable criteria, but on the judgment, sensibility, or bias of the historian. The great methodological gain from breaking the problem down into distinct categories of preconditions, precipitants and triggers is that the historian is relieved of the futile, and intellectually dishonest, task of trying to arrange all the causes in a single rank order. He is no longer called on, for example, to decide whether or not the obstinacy and duplicity of Charles I was more important than the spread of Puritanism in causing the Revolution. Each set of causes can be handled separately in its own category, while since the categories themselves follow sequentially one from another they do not need to be measured against each other.

2. The preconditions, 1529-1629

The instability of the Tudor polity

If one looks, with all the wisdom of hindsight, at the structure of the Tudor polity in its heyday during the first twenty-five years of the reign of Elizabeth, that age of relative tranquillity before the storm clouds began to gather in the late 1580s, one can see that it was essentially unstable. This is not the place to re-open the question of what the Early Tudors were striving to achieve. Was it no more than an efficient bureaucracy at the centre and a political balance summed up by the concept of sovereignty residing in a 'King in Parliament'? Or was the Spanish Ambassador nearer to the mark when in 1498 he reported home that Henry VII 'would like to govern England in the French fashion, but he cannot'.[32] There are good reasons for believing that Henry VII, and more particularly Henry VIII, cast envious eyes across the Channel, and were only too anxious to acquire those powers upon which were founded the strong Renaissance monarchies of Europe. It was Henry VIII who bluntly told the Irish 'of our absolute power we be above the law', and Edward Lord Herbert in the seventeenth century seems to have had a shrewder idea of the Early Tudors' real attitude towards the law than some twentieth-century historians, who are more easily impressed by conformity to the letter than by allegiance to the spirit. Lord Herbert remarked of Henry VII that 'He used to take their [the common lawyers'] advice obliquely, and no otherwise than to discover how safe his own designs were, and so with less danger to vary from them. Which deviations yet he would so regulate, as that his actions at home had still, if not their ground, yet at least their pretext from the Common Law.'[33] After many years in which it has not been respectable to use the phrase in academic circles, the concept of 'Tudor despotism', as an aspiration if not a reality, is at last becoming something that can be talked about again.[34] It is arguable that between 1470 and 1558, and particularly between 1529 and 1547, there was in England a desire in official quarters to acquire some of the tools for strong monarchical government; that Henry VIII was not by nature and inclination a constitutional monarch, but a powerful autocrat working perforce through legal and constitutional channels to acquire new sources of authority. In the 1530s the King and his advisers extended the definition of treason to cover the spoken word, seized the enormous wealth of the monasteries, dominated the universities, strengthened and codified the powers of the prerogative courts, absorbed Wales into the English administrative and legal system, crushed a revolt in the North and subordinated it at last to control from London, declared the monarch head of the Church, attempted to extend the legal authority of proclamations in a way we can only guess at, but which certainly aroused bitter hostility in Parliament, and toyed with plans for a standing army.

This drive towards absolutism faltered and then came to a halt, partly because of the survival of powerful medieval institutions and political traditions, notably in the common law and in Parliament, and partly because neither the King nor his leading minister devoted themselves single-mindedly to the task. An equally important reason, however, was the fortuitous one that too much had to be done in too short a time. The Crown had barely mastered the medieval feudal nobility, improved its shaky finances and restored some semblance of law and order, than it was faced with the problems of the Reformation. The absolute necessity for legitimation and popular backing for the break with Rome forced the King into active consultation with Parliament, whether he liked it or not. So long as Parliament was co-operative, the process increased the legislative power of the executive. But the crisis deepened in the early 1540s with the growing rift between two religiously-oriented aristocratic factions, at which point the Crown took the fatal step of diverting its political energies and dissipating its financial resources in a major foreign war with France from 1543 to 1551. The fact that this war was peculiarly futile in its ends – the capture of a single port town, Boulogne – and peculiarly wasteful of its means, merely adds to the historical paradox of a pointless adventure which may have helped to change the course of English history.[35] By the time it was over, the Crown had sold or given away the bulk of the monastic and chantry property, the governing class was split between two competing fanaticisms, and the mercenary force needed for the assertion of royal absolutism had been disbanded for lack of funds. Parliament was increasingly asserting its independence, now based securely upon its power of the purse and the need for its legislative assistance in obtaining a religious settlement. After 1558 Elizabeth and her advisers abandoned all ambitions to develop a continental-style monarchy, and settled down to manage the political institutions as they found them. Unfortunately for themselves, the system they inherited was a peculiarly brittle one.

To argue along these lines does not at all imply that any society which is not founded on a substantial degree of consensus is liable to disintegration. The structural-functionalists among sociologists and political scientists have seriously underestimated both the degree of conflict and the number of largely obsolete or dysfunctional institutions which exist in any society and can be absorbed without too much discomfort. Right up to the early nineteenth century our ancestors tolerated a level of casual personal violence, and a degree of public disorder, which would be completely unacceptable in a civilized society today. On the other hand, the Tudor State lacked the brute force to beat down opposition, and only temporarily enjoyed the united support that would make such force unnecessary. When the élites began to quarrel, either the structure would have to change, or the whole edifice would begin to totter and shudder under the strain.

The Elizabethan State was remarkably deficient in some of the essential components of power. Let us begin with money, the sinews of all government. This was a problem which the early Tudors seemed to be on the verge of solving. In 1522, for the first time in nearly one hundred years, and the last time for more than one hundred years, a new and relatively honest assessment was carried out to form the basis for a Parliamentary tax on property.

Moreover the customs revenue soared as trade increased, and a revived fiscal feudalism squeezed wealth out of the landed classes.[36] Most important of all, however, was the fact that between 1536 and 1552 the Crown laid hands on the vast property of monasteries and chantries, usually reckoned (without much hard statistical evidence) to amount to at least a quarter of the country.[37] Had this property been retained and exploited, both for the wealth it could produce and for the political and religious patronage it carried with it, it could have provided the State with overwhelming resources, which would have made it virtually independent of Parliamentary taxation. But before it had even been assimilated and absorbed, the bulk of the property was sold off to pay for war, so that by 1562 the Crown was left with an independent income which with a tight rein on expenditure was just sufficient, but no more than sufficient, for peace-time purposes.[38] At the first hint of war, the Crown was obliged to go cap in hand to Parliament for funds.

Having deprived itself of the financial and political benefits of confiscated church property, the Crown failed to develop those alternative sources of revenue which were so important to other European powers. Monopoly of an essential mineral was one. Alum was a prime support of the Papacy, gold and silver of Spain, salt of France, and copper of Sweden. The adverse decision by the common law judges in the case of the Earl of Northumberland in 1568 deprived the English Crown of its chance to make a profit from the almost limitless reserves of England's coal and non-precious metals. It tried to exploit first copper and then salt and alum, but failed to make a profit from any of them.[39]

The second great resource of continental States was the sale of offices in administration and the law. But the English bureaucracy remained pitifully small, and Elizabeth's effort to increase the number of legal offices was defeated by the judges in the Cavendish Case in 1587. Moreover such offices as existed were bought and sold by the officials and courtiers themselves with no benefit accruing to the Crown.[40] (James I entered the field late, in 1616, but the profits he reaped failed to compensate for the unpopularity he earned.) Equally serious was the fact that the administrative weakness of monarchy, and its consequent reliance on the gentry and the merchants for support, rendered it unable – or unwilling – to adjust old taxes to new conditions. The Elizabethan administration put political goodwill before fiscal efficiency, and as a result failed to adjust revenues to cope with inflation or to tax new wealth. The

Book of Rates, which declared the value of goods for customs, was only altered once in eighty years, despite the steady rise in import prices, while receipts from wardship actually declined, and assessments for Parliamentary subsidies were left unchanged. By 1603 the propertied classes had become accustomed to avoiding taxation, and efforts by the Stuarts to tighten things up and to tax the rich at a realistic level by means of impositions, fines for wardship, forced loans or ship money inevitably ran into serious legal and political obstacles.[41] The early Stuart monarchy was financially boxed in at all points, since it could only achieve fiscal solvency and the equitable distribution of the tax burden at the cost of a political crisis.

If it lacked money, the English monarchy also lacked troops. In the 1530s some elements in government had been considering a scheme for the creation of a large standing army financed out of confiscated Church wealth, and in the 1540s a considerable force of Italian and German mercenaries had been stationed on English soil.[42] They effectively crushed the peasant revolts of 1549, but they were paid off in 1551 as an economy measure. Thereafter the Crown had to rely upon a poorly-armed and poorly-trained local militia, a tiny personal bodyguard, and in emergencies a rallying of the traditional forces of the magnates and their retainers, tenants and servants.[43] The Tudor and Stuart kings were in no position to mount a large-scale offensive against internal rebels without voluntary military support from its own subjects.

To strengthen its judicial authority, the Crown set up a series of new courts to exercise powers of justice and of administration over certain geographical areas (Wales, the North, the West), certain categories of people (Wards, Exchequer) and certain categories of offences (Star Chamber, Requests, Admiralty). These courts were more subjected to royal controls than the common law courts, their procedures were swifter and cheaper, and their officials were more concerned with the firm administration of justice than with the preservation of obsolete legal archaisms. But the common law courts survived, and with them common law traditions, which were to play a large part in the coming political struggles.[44]

In the first half the sixteenth century the government succeeded in creating a unified central administration with the Lord Treasurer at the head, and the Privy Council as the main executive body. This was the work not of Thomas Cromwell, at whose death the Crown was left with a chaotic tangle of rival financial agencies, but of his successors who firmly restored the central fiscal authority of the revived Exchequer. But even now anomalies persisted, such as the independent Court of Wards, and old-fashioned officials went on fighting long-drawn-out and often successful inter-departmental battles to the detriment of efficiency.[45]

Far more serious, however, was the failure of the government even to attempt to establish more than a skeleton bureaucracy of its own in the towns and the countryside. The reason for this failure is still obscure, largely because historians have not asked themselves why it was that the so-called 'administrative revolution' of the early sixteenth century was confined to Westminster. What seems to have happened was that the early Tudors deliberately built up the authority of the gentry as a means of destroying the local power bases of their over-mighty subjects, the great territorial magnates of the late middle ages. These men had constructed the most formidable monopolies of local power and privilege and patronage, by which the gentry of the region had become almost wholly dependent upon their good lordship, rather than upon that of the King.[46] The destruction of these local monopolies was a much more difficult and delicate task, and far more important in its effects in strengthening royal authority than the improvements in the central administration machinery, the so-called Tudor revolution in government, of which so much has recently been heard. The full details of the process, which involved undermining magnate authority by building up a class of rich gentry dependent on the Crown for advancement and power, has been worked out in convincing detail for the North of England, where the situation was at its most acute.[47]

The old nobility had not yet been fully brought to heel however, when the Crown's attention was diverted to other problems, the Reformation in the 1530s and the war and inflation in the 1540s. As has been seen, the result was to make the Crown heavily dependent on Parliament for political and financial support. The classes represented in the House of Commons were willing enough to give the King their support in his religious and political policies, but only so long as they were left to rule over the countryside and the towns. The Crown was thus in no position to proceed to the next stage in the creation of a strong monarchy, the replacement of the local gentry by paid officials of its own. As a result there was a tacit agreement to divide responsibility, and the main burden of local administration had to be left in the hands of unpaid gentry and urban worthies, whose loyalty and efficiency was dependent on a careful regard being had for their interests, privileges, and prejudices.[48] So far from being progressively weakened, local particularism grew step by step with the growth of the central government.

To counteract these centrifugal tendencies, Henry VIII, after he had broken with Rome for reasons of dynastic security, did his utmost to create a self-consciously national Church which would unify the country around the King. Despite ferocious treason and heresy laws, he failed in the attempt, largely because he lacked the administrators to enforce his will. Once he had started on the Reformation, Henry found himself riding on the back of a tiger; he could neither control its movements nor jump off as it plunged ahead. Much as he might have wished to adhere to relatively orthodox Catholic doctrine, the logic of politics and the pressures of a growing public opinion forced him in an erratic but ultimately irresistible Protestant direction. He could hardly break with Rome without challenging the spiritual supremacy of the heirs of St Peter. He could hardly suppress the monasteries without rejecting the ideals of chastity and poverty for which they stood; nor could he seize the jewels and precious metals from the shrines of saints without denying the value of the intercession of saints and the adoration of their relics; nor could he prepare to suppress the chantries without rejecting prayers for the dead and the notion of Purgatory. However much he might back and fill, blow hot and cold, terrorize both flanks by gestures such as burning three Protestants for heresy and hanging two Catholics for treason on the same day, the pressure of events inexorably carried England towards a fragmentation of religious unity.

The subsequent extreme religious oscillations of the reigns of Edward VI and Mary, each imposed on a reluctant and bewildered population by a tiny minority of zealots, only deepened the confusion and threatened religious anarchy. Clergymen married their housekeepers, then were forcibly separated from their wives;[49] they changed from a Catholic mass service in Latin to a Zwinglian communion service in English, and back again. In the 1520s church wardens had spent large sums painting biblical scenes on the walls of their churches and adding new images of saints; in 1549 they whitewashed the walls and removed the rood-lofts; in 1553 they hastily put them back again; and in 1560 they tore them down again. The official Elizabethan policy was to bolster up the unconvincing political compromise of the Anglican church with a lukewarm and a cynical Erastianism. It was certainly successful in cooling religious passions and avoiding an outbreak of doctrinal warfare linked to rival aristocratic factions. But it was not designed – indeed by its very nature it could not be made – to satisfy the needs of a population that was starved of spiritual nourishment. The hungry flock were obliged to look elsewhere. Even one of its principle architects, Sir William Cecil, admitted that the more zealous Protestants were bound to regard it as 'a cloaked papistry or a mingle-mangle'.[50] The lack of a firm doctrinal base for the official Church prevented the development of any assertive self-confidence or missionary zeal. Few could believe it could last, and fewer still could rally enthusiastically around a church which could not even make up its mind about the nature of the sacrament. Symbolic of the aspirations – and the weakness – of the Elizabethan Church was the removal of the figure of Christ on the cross on the rood-screen of many a country church, and its replacement by the royal coat of arms. Coupled with the half-heartedness of its persecution of dissidents, this apathy permitted – indeed made inevitable – the development of substantial and influential groups of enthusiastic nonconformists to the left and to the right, Puritans and Catholics. Moreover, in the 1540s and 1550s the Crown had absent-mindedly given away or sold to the laity the patronage of many Church livings along with the estates of the monasteries, a move which in retrospect can be seen to have had fateful consequences. It meant that appointment of most clergy was controlled not by the State or the Church but by the individual lay landlords. Neither the King nor the bishops were masters in their own clerical house.

This weakness on the religious front was compounded by equally serious weaknesses in social structure. The over-mighty subjects of the late middle ages had been largely, if not entirely, eliminated by 1540, thanks to a royal policy of attainders and confiscations which was powerfully assisted by natural demographic attrition. But in order to secure local and national support for the Reformation settlement and a dynastic succession, Henry felt obliged to replace these magnates with a new official and military aristocracy established as great territorial landlords on the ruins of the monasteries and the old nobility. The classic example of this process is the creation of the Russells, Earls of Bedford, as great West Country magnates in order to maintain Court control over a remote and dangerous area.[51] This was all very well at the time, but it opened up the possibility that one day the heirs of these noblemen might turn this power and patronage against the Crown. Moreover, no sooner had this new Henrician aristocracy been created than the financial pressures generated by the wars of the 1540s forced the Crown to sell off further large parts of the newly acquired Church property. Either directly or by resale this property came into the hands of local yeoman and gentry, thus creating a squirarchy whose aspirations and interests would eventually have to be accommodated somehow or other within the political system.[52]

To conclude this catalogue of weaknesses, potential or actual, the government had inadequate control over the written and spoken word. Censorship of the press was firmly established by law, but its effectiveness was weakened by aristocratic protection of puritan pamphleteers, the smuggling of books from abroad, and the operation of clandestine printing presses in England.[53] The most important propaganda instrument of the day was the pulpit, but the loss of patronage of many livings to the laity, which was itself divided, meant that there was never a time when some preachers were not urging upon their congregations ideas which were displeasing and even dangerous to the government. Moreover, the grammar schools and universities were also filled with teachers whose sympathies with the Established Church were less than absolute.[54] In an age of ideological conflict, this lack of firm control of the media of communication was a very serious handicap to a government.

All these weaknesses might not have mattered so much, had there not survived from the medieval past a powerful national representative body, which after a bitter struggle in the early sixteenth century (the full story of which has not yet been told) had succeeded in preserving for itself the essential powers to consent to taxation and to vote on legislation.[55] Over against this was set the ill-defined authority of the so-called 'prerogative', and the increasingly charismatic nature of Renaissance kingship. The Holbein portrait of Henry VIII, arms akimbo and legs astride like a colossus, perfectly expresses the image of the new monarchy.[56] Elizabeth inherited something of her father's irritable and authoritarian temperament, together with his capacity for charm when she cared to exercise it, so that it is hardly surprising first that she had serious trouble with her Parliaments from the moment she ascended the throne, and second that she usually managed to get her own way in the short run.[57] But day to day tactical agility was no substitute for the creation of a concensus on basic strategic policies and on the constitutional division of responsibilities.

In 1671 the architect of the Restoration of Charles II, George Monck, Duke of Albermarle, published 'Some Directions for the

Preventing of Civil Wars'. He laid down four principles, the first three of which were reliable control of strategic fortresses, 'one religion in the State' and a 'rich public treasure', while the fourth was the diversion, occupation and control of the hopeless poor.[58] By Monck's standards, the Elizabethan political structure was inadequate. Whether one looks at its political support, financial resources, military and administrative power, social cohesion, legal subordination, religious unity, or control of propaganda, it appears to be shot through with contradictions and weaknesses. It is to the development of these contradictions and weaknesses over the seventy years from 1559 to 1629 that attention must now be directed.

The development of disequilibrium, 1529-1629

Economic growth

Since one of the most important political developments was the growing inability of the state to adjust to new social forces, it seems logical to begin with the economic changes which generated those forces. In the first place there was a very significant increase both in population and in total economic resources which began in about 1520. The doubling of the population in the 120 years before the civil war is the critical variable of the period, an event the ramifications of which spread out into every aspect of the society and was causally related to major changes in agriculture, trade, industry, urbanization, education, social mobility and overseas settlement.[59] It gave a tremendous stimulous to agricultural output, which increased sufficiently fast between 1500 and 1660 to feed twice the number of mouths, although undoubtedly at a reduced standard of living. The lot of the poor may have deteriorated, but England managed to avoid those massive demographic crises which tore apart the social fabric of northern France every thirty years or so until the early eighteenth century. This remarkable achievement was partly a result of an expansion of the area under cultivation, eating into the wastes, the forests, the hillsides and even the fens. But it was also a result of improvements in agricultural techniques: 'up and down husbandry', better fertilization, more drainage, the floating of water meadows, improved crop rotation, more scientific stock breeding, and new feed crops. There is some little evidence to suggest that in some areas the ratio of crop yield to seed sown per acre very significantly increased between the fifteenth and the mid-seventeenth centuries.[60] This expansion of agricultural output could only be achieved, however, at the cost of upsetting the former social balance. On the land there was a massive shift away from a feudal and paternalist relationship between landlord and tenant, towards one more exclusively based on the maximization of profits in a market economy. In the sixteenth century the combination of rapidly rising food prices and stagnant rents shifted the distribution of agricultural profits away from the landlord and towards the tenant. In the early seventeenth century rents increased more rapidly than prices, and profits flowed back to the landlord and away from the tenant. This shift to economic rents was accompanied by a reorganization of property rights, by which more and more land fell into private control through enclosures of both waste and common fields. As a result of this process and of the engrossing of farms into larger units of production, there began to emerge the tripartite pattern of later English rural society, landlord, prosperous tenant farmer, and landless labourer. These changes were essential to feed the additional mouths, but tens of thousands of small-holders were driven off the land or reduced to wage labourers while others found their economic position undermined by encroachment on, or overstocking of, the common lands by the big farmers and the landlords. The enclosure became a popular scapegoat for the dislocations inevitable in so major a redistribution and reallocation of the land, but there can be no doubt that the extra millions of Englishmen were only fed at the cost of much individual hardship suffered by many of the small peasantry.

Although overseas trade did not expand very much between 1551 and 1604, it grew rapidly thereafter, and it enormously diversified its markets and its sources of imports in preparation for the more startling growth of the late seventeenth century.[61] It expanded into the Baltic and the Mediterranean, and especially to India and the Americas. Powerful joint-stock companies sprang up, which were soon to demand influence on foreign policy. So important had foreign trade become to the national economy that a trade slump had repercussions in every sector of society, and for the first time came to dominate the political scene and be the main preoccupation of Parliament and the Executive. The cloth trade in particular was a powerful unifying force in society since its prosperity affected the landed classes, who owned the sheep which produced the wool, the poor labourers and their wives and children, who spun it, the artisans who wove it, the clothiers who handled it, and the merchants who exported it. As Thomas Middleton remarked in 1622, 'The Clothing or Drapery of the Kingdom . . . is of very high consequence, and concerneth both the sovereign and the subject, noble and ignoble, even all sorts and callings and conditions of men in this commonwealth . . . This is . . . a bond to knit the subjects together in their several societies.'[62] This identity of economic interest between the landed classes, the artisans and the merchant community was the principal force which united the opposition around such issues as taxation, impositions, monopolies, and foreign policy, and which made it very difficult for the Crown to play one group off against another. As a result the gentry in Parliament in 1621 were intensely preoccupied with the depression in the cloth trade, and by 1650 England was fighting the first purely commercial war in its history, against its Dutch rivals.

Other aspects of England's economic growth fostered national unity and stimulated capitalist enterprise, both of which increased the importance attached to the economic policies of the Crown, and eventually brought them under criticism. Internal trade greatly increased in order to supply the growing population, and was assisted by the organization of regular carriers on the main roads, the growth of specialized markets, and a proliferation of pedlars and hucksters operating out of inns.[63] This development of internal trade was enormously helped by the fact that there were hardly any internal tolls on rivers or roads or at the entry into towns. This fortunate legacy from the medieval past put England in a unique position relative to the rest of Europe, where internal trade was clogged by a proliferation of tolls and levies at every turn. Another important development was the shift from a position in which interest on capital was legally forbidden – and in fact obtainable only at exorbitant rates – to one in which money could be borrowed on terms that compare favourably with those of any place and period, including our own. In the thirty years between 1620 and 1650 interest rates fell from 10 per cent to 5 per cent, which meant that English entrepreneurs (and English spendthrifts) could now borrow money at rates which were equal to any in Europe except the Dutch.[64] This dramatic reduction in interest rates was both cause and consequence of the growth of fluid capital, and the development of institutional facilities for its employment such as joint-stock companies and deposit banking with scriveners and goldsmiths. It was also a consequence of the growing readiness of the landed classes to lend their money at interest, and the very modest amount of capital, compared with other countries, which was soaked up by investment in the purchase of government offices and government *rentes*.

The main industrial activity of England remained the manufacture and processing of cloth, catering for a large domestic and export market, but there were none the less some significant new developments in the century after 1540. Coal-mining in the Newcastle area became the first really large-scale bulk-producing industry in the western world, while in a host of other industries, from wire-making to soap-boiling, England took over the technological lead from Germany. The result of this new industrial activity in terms of capital invested, the value of goods produced, and the amount of labour employed, was small in relation to the economy as a whole, and it is an exaggeration to speak of a 'first industrial revolution'.[65] England in the seventeenth century remained what it and the rest of Europe had always been, an under-developed society. On the other hand there can be no doubt that it was much more permeated with small-scale industry and commerce, much more market-oriented, and much richer than it had ever been before, more so than any other contemporary society, with the probable exception of the United Provinces. It is hardly surprising that in the Grand Remonstrance of 1641, that great catch-all of parliamentary grievances against the Crown, a good deal of prominence is given to the evils of royal economic policies and monopolies, and to the damage done to trade and industry by fiscal exactions of dubious legality.

An important aspect of the economic growth of the sixteenth and early seventeenth centuries was its concentration on the capital city of London. The city grew by leaps and bounds from about 60,000 in 1500 to about 450,000 in 1640. Its proportion of the total population of England and Wales grew from about $2\frac{1}{2}$ per cent to about 8 per cent, and at a time when it boasted of half a million inhabitants, no other town in the country had more than about 25,000.[66] A very high proportion of the surplus labour created by the demographic growth of the countryside ended up in London. The city was also the principal overseas trading centre in the country, and by virtue of its location and the grip obtained by the monopolistic trading companies, an overwhelmingly large proportion of English commerce flowed through its docks. By 1550, 90 per cent of England's principal export commodity, namely cloth, passed through London, and this stranglehold was successfully maintained through the commercial expansion and reorientation of the seventeenth century. In 1700

London handled 80 per cent of English exports and 70 per cent of her imports, a situation which was probably little different from that sixty years before, on the eve of the Revolution.[67] The centralization of the law courts on Westminster Hall and of the barristers on the Inns of Court meant that London was almost the only place for litigation, while a decreasingly peripatetic Court attracted more and more clients and suitors around the old palace at Westminster. By the mid-seventeenth century London dominated the national scene as no other capital city in Europe, not even Paris. The enormous concentration of economic resources, political influences, professional expertise and population created a situation in which the control of the city meant in considerable measure control of many of the levers of power. If the Crown were to lose the city, as it did in 1641, it lost military, financial and political resources on a major scale. A French king could and did survive the loss of Paris, but it was far more difficult for an English king to survive the loss of London.

It can hardly be an accident that the first of the 'Great Revolutions' in the history of the West should have occurred in one of the two societies in which proto-capitalism was most highly developed. In no other major country were the relations between landlord and tenant so much governed by the laws of the market place rather than by customary relationships of service; in no other country had private property rights encroached so extensively on the commercial rights of the village, and had the consolidation of private holdings progressed so far. In few had there developed such extensive rural industries, as in areas such as Gloucestershire, where a substantial proportion of the work-force was engaged, full or part-time, in industrial and distributive trades.[68] In none was there an extractive industry on the scale of the Newcastle coal mines. In none was there a capital city so large in proportion to the national population or with so concentrated an array of facilities and activities as mid-seventeenth century London. In none were the landed classes so extensively involved in investments in overseas trade and settlement, even if the sums they contributed were relatively small. In few or none were the great landowners more actively engaged in exploiting the mineral resources of their land or in developing their urban properties.

It is not possible to demonstrate a causal relationship in terms of a clash of clear-cut economic interests between these developments and the breakdown of the *ancien régime* of the Stuarts. It is not possible, for example, to support claims that the entrepreneurial classes, industrialists and merchants, supported Parliament. There is no evidence whatever that the alignment of forces in 1642 split the country along these lines. What can be said, however, is that these economic developments were dissolving old bonds of service and obligation and creating new relationships founded on the operations of the market, and that the domestic and foreign policies of the Stuarts were failing to respond to these changing circumstances. Much of the political friction of the early seventeenth century was generated by resentments, jealousies and tensions arising from the rise to wealth of new social groups and the decline of others, and by the fumbling and corrupt way in which the administration handled the changing situation. Many things were restored at the Restoration, but it is surely significant that among those which were not were feudal tenures, restraints upon enclosure of land, such monopolies and economic controls as did not suit the convenience of influential interest groups, and a foreign policy which gave little weight to commercial objectives.

Social change

If this analysis is correct, attention should be directed less to the absolute increase of wealth, changes in the way it was earned, and its geographical concentration than to the consequential changes in the numerical proportions of the various orders and strata of the society and their share of the national income.[69] The central fact about English social history between 1540 and 1640, and in consequence of English political history, was the growth in numbers and wealth of the landed classes and the professions. The number of peers rose from 60 to 160; baronets and knights from 500 to 1400; esquires from perhaps 800 to 3,000; and armigerous gentry from perhaps 5,000 to 15,000. The landed classes thus trebled in numbers at a time when the population scarcely doubled.[70] Everywhere gentlemen were acquiring substantial holdings of land and were building for themselves a country seat. The house served as a home for family and household, as a centre for the administration of a landed estate, and as a political power base from which to dominate the locality. The expansion in the number of J.P.s during this period – from 23 to 58 between 1558 and 1662 in Hertfordshire, for example – was not merely a measure to provide more efficient local government: it was also recognition of the great expansion in the number of the eligible local élite.[71]

This numerical expansion was made possible mainly by the transfer of huge quantities of landed property first from the Church to the Crown and then from the Crown to the laity, mostly gentry, in a series of massive sales to pay for foreign wars. In the hundred years between 1536 and 1636 the Crown threw on to the market land – its own patrimony and that recently seized from the Church – which sold for about £6½ million at 1630 prices.[72] Since much of the property was sold at an artificially low figure due to under-rating by corrupt or incompetent officials, the true value must have been significantly higher.[73] The more one reflects upon English history in the sixteenth and seventeenth centuries the more important appears this seizure and redistribution of Church property. The land market was becoming more active before the property came up for sale, but its disposal in huge quantities in the twenty-five years from 1538 to 1563 transformed the situation. All the evidence suggests that the volume of property transactions doubled in a decade, and that this acceleration, coupled with the easing of legal restrictions with the Statute of Wills in 1540, created a psychological climate in which it was no longer considered immoral to sell land.[74] The result was eighty years of extensive activity in the land market, meaning eighty years of unprecedented social mobility among the landed classes. The second result was the passage of a great deal of land, and with it Church patronage, from institutional to private hands, resulting in the creation of a much more numerous and more politically and religiously influential gentry class. Furthermore, although the aristocracy gained a good deal of Church property by purchase or gift immediately after the dissolution of the monasteries, a lot of it was resold to the gentry in the late sixteenth century.[75] At the same time many small copyholders and leaseholders were being squeezed by inflated prices and rising rents, and were being bought out by gentry and rich yeoman. The tide of land was flowing towards the gentry from both ends of the social spectrum.

The increase in the number of the gentry was accompanied by a striking increase in their real income and in their accumulation of capital and consumption goods. Proof of this affluence is to be seen in the explosion of architectural construction – the biggest boom in country-house building in English history – and in the appearance of more, and more luxurious, furniture and equipment in contemporary inventories. One estimate reckons that the average value of the net personal estate of gentry in Warwickshire, adjusted to allow for the price inflation, increased by a factor of 3½ to 4. In other words the standard of living of the average gentry in this area increased by nearly 400 per cent between the 1530s and the 1630s.[76]

This cheerful picture of growing numbers and growing prosperity must be shaded to include the fact that many gentry were declining while others were rising, and that many of the poorer gentry were only just managing to maintain their status and position. It is also important to stress the difference between the rich and powerful squirarchy, the few dominant families in each county, and the mass of smaller 'parish gentry,' whose outlook and aspirations were far more restricted. Even so, the houses and the inventories of the latter indicate that, despite their complaints and their debts, they were in fact living a good deal more comfortably in 1640 than their ancestors had lived in 1540. In a number of cases their expectations may have exceeded reality, and some of them were certainly running into debt and selling up. But after taking this declining gentry element into account, the fact remains that the overall position of the gentry class, both at the top and the lower levels, was unmistakably and strikingly improving. Both relatively and absolutely there was an impressive rise of the gentry as a status group in terms of numbers and wealth, whatever fluctuations there may have been in the fortunes of some of the individual families who composed it.

The increase in the wealth and numbers of the gentry would have had only limited political consequences had it not been for a third development, a profound shift in attitude towards the local magnates on the one hand and the state on the other. There was a sea-change in men's ideas of loyalty, resulting from the decline of aristocratic power and influence.[77] The hold of nobles over client gentry and tenantry was weakened because of the increasing absenteeism of the former, and the shift to economic rents, which severely reduced the service element in landlord-tenant relationships. The process was greatly accelerated by the persistent activity of the central government, which was seeping steadily into the remote areas, subsuming local loyalties under allegiance to itself, wearing down the recalcitrant by administrative and legal pressure, and cowing the rebellious by the sheer scale of its resources. Education at school replaced education in a noble household; service in local government as J.P. or commissioner replaced service in the household administration of a local magnate. In the short run, the decline of the influence of the aristocracy meant increased dependence of the gentry on the Crown; in the long run, however, it meant the liberation of the gentry from the influence of either noble or Crown. By 1640 the gentry were neither faithful retainers of a local earl nor obedient servants of the political faction in control of power at Court. They were full citizens of the commonwealth, independent men of substance. They were pouring into the universities and the Inns of Court, they were filling up the numbers on the bench of Justices, and they were crowding out the other social groups in the House of Commons. They were a force to be reckoned with, and any government which thwarted their interests or affronted their beliefs and values was likely to run into serious political trouble. In the reign of Henry VIII these men expressed their disapproval of royal policies by staging a local rebellion like the Pilgrimage of Grace, which was doomed to defeat and indeed was hardly intended to be much more than a gesture of protest.[78] In the reign of Charles I they expressed their disapproval by blocking local administration, and demanding redress of grievances on the floor of the House of Commons.

The rise of the gentry, interpreted as something a good deal more profound and complicated than merely a redistribution of economic resources, is politically the single most important social development of the age.[79] The rise of the professional classes is none the less not far behind it. The most numerous, wealthy and influential professional group was the lawyers, whose numbers increased dramatically, until by 1688 Gregory King could reckon that the entire legal profession amounted to 10,000 persons. Many of them were struggling attorneys and solicitors on the fringes of middle-class respectability, but many others were wealthy London barristers and legal officials. The calls to the bar rose by 40 per cent between the 1590s and the 1630s, and the more successful members of the profession accumulated huge fortunes. The medical profession underwent a similar expansion, while the more fashionable practitioners were making fortunes unheard of in previous periods.[80]

The third important group whose wealth and influence were on the increase were the merchants, especially the merchant élites of London and the major provincial cities like Exeter, Bristol and Newcastle. Their grip on the trade and the political power of the towns increased as time went on, and there is strong evidence of their growing wealth and self-confidence.[81]

In short, what happened between 1540 and 1640 was a massive shift of relative wealth away from Church and Crown, and away from both the very rich and the very poor towards the upper middle and middle classes. The shift was caused on the one hand by land sales and monopoly concessions by a government hard-pressed to pay for war, by the inflation of prices, and by improvident expenditure patterns maintained by the old rich; and on the other by the entrepreneurial activities of the new rich and the growing demand for professional services of an increasingly sophisticated society. This changing socio-economic balance, coupled with the rise of Puritanism and the spread of education, meant that there was bound to be friction between the traditional wielders of power, the Crown, courtiers, higher clergy and aristocracy, and the growing but as yet far from homogeneous forces of gentry, lawyers, merchants, yeomen and small tradesmen. The problem that faced the state was how to bring the latter into fruitful and co-operative participation in the political process.

Decline of external threats

Men of wealth and property allowed this problem to reach the stage of open conflict between Parliament and the King in the early years of the seventeenth century, primarily because they were no longer afraid, or rather were no longer as afraid as they had been. During the whole of the last half of the sixteenth century the ruling élites had been held together by a triple fear of a *jacquerie* of the poor, a civil war over a disputed succession linked to religious divisions, and an invasion by foreign enemies. By the early seventeenth century, however, all these fears had considerably abated. The last peasant revolt serious enough to send the gentry fleeing from their homes in terror had been in 1549, when risings had taken place all over southern England.[82] Brutal repression quickly snuffed out the fires of rebellion in all but the one county of Norfolk, but memories of this alarming experience died hard, and were almost certainly a stimulus to the enforcement, such as it was, of anti-enclosure legislation. But by 1640 two generations had gone by since the great fear, and memories had grown dim. Moreover, the threat of a renewed outbreak on a large scale, though certainly possible, now seemed fairly remote. Population growth had eased off, real wages had stabilized or even risen a little, and labour-saving enclosure for pasture was being replaced by labour-intensive enclosure for arable. Last but not least, a national poor relief system was now in operation, along with a certain amount of private charity, to take care of the old, the sick, and the growing numbers of unemployed. This system of national tax-supported poor relief, which got under way on a systematic scale in about 1600 and grew steadily in scope and cost thereafter, was one of the more important single differences between England and the Continent.[83] As early as the seventeenth century, England was a welfare state and not too inhumane a one at that. For reasons we do not fully understand, the English propertied classes realized very early on that the financial cost of poor relief was a small price to pay for the domestic tranquillity and social deference which resulted. The welfare system was the only viable alternative to a local bureaucracy and a standing army as an instrument for social control.

Another of the things which made England so different from Europe was the extraordinary lightness of the burden of taxation placed on the poor, most of whom were altogether exempt. They therefore lacked the main grievance which both reduced their contemporaries in France to abject misery and stimulated them to ferocious rebellion against an oppressive state. Consequently, although some minor risings took place in the 1630s in old forest areas like Wiltshire, they were severely localized and never seemed very threatening.[84] In 1642 men of property talked of the danger of popular uprising in order to discourage each other from taking up arms, but they did not take it sufficiently seriously for it to deter them. On the very eve of the outbreak of open war, Simonds D'Ewes vainly warned his fellow members of Parliament: 'We know not what advantage the meaner sort also may take to divide the spoils of the rich and noble among them'. The looting of the houses of some Catholic noblemen in East Anglia by undisciplined mobs seemed evidence that D'Ewes' prophecy was coming true. It has even been argued that the Parliamentary Ordinance for the raising of troops – in practice against the King – was accepted by the Suffolk gentry as a guarantee of the maintenance of internal order.[85] But too much cannot be made of all this, and the willingness of the gentry and nobility to resort to war in 1642 stands in contrast to the situation in 1688, when mob violence was quite widespread, and was clearly influential in persuading the men of property to close ranks and to unite rapidly behind William III.[86]

The second fear which persisted throughout the whole of the reign of Elizabeth was that her death would unleash a civil war over a disputed succession complicated by religious rivalries. This fear was a very real one, and it haunted politicians and Members of Parliament for forty-five years. The persistent efforts of Privy Councillors and the House of Commons to persuade Elizabeth either to marry and beget an heir or else to declare her successor—efforts made in flat defiance of the royal will – is proof of how seriously they regarded the threat to national security. The fear receded a little after Mary Queen of Scots had been executed, but it lay just beneath the surface of the Cecil–Essex feud in the 1590s, and burst out into the open when Elizabeth lay dying in 1603. Londoners frantically bought weapons and hoarded food, while one enterprising scholar prepared himself to be the historian of a civil war which never happened.[87] The peaceful accession of James finally put these anxieties to rest, but it should be remembered that his son, Charles I, was the first English monarch since Henry VIII to ascend to the throne with a fully undisputed title.

Elizabeth's policy of masterly inactivity and politic temporizing was a brilliant success in so far as it staved off the civil wars which were tearing apart large areas of contemporary Europe, most notably England's nearest neighbours, France and the Low Countries. On the other hand, none of the problems facing the society were resolved, but merely postponed, to come to a head in a more dangerous form later on, while the very fact of Elizabeth's success had the paradoxical result of making civil war more rather than less likely in the future. The avoidance of an explosion for over a century lulled the English élites into a false sense of security, and they were therefore more willing to risk armed confrontation in 1642. The contrast with the 1680s, when the political nation again reached a deadlock soluble only by war, cannot be more striking. 'No doubt there might have been a revolution in 1681, if the memories of 1642 had been less vivid. The lesson of 1642, however, had been thoroughly learned: Revolution meant social upheaval, insecurity of life and property, and military despotism.'[88] As a result, the landed and urban élites drew back, Shaftesbury fled into exile, and the crisis passed. Thanks to the very success of Elizabeth in avoiding civil war, the propertied classes in 1642 had no such experience behind them from which to draw the lessons of moderation and compromise.

The third fear was that of invasion from abroad, but by the early seventeenth century this too had greatly diminished, and indeed had all but vanished. The danger of invasion from Spain, which had been so real under Elizabeth, finally disappeared with the peace of 1604. The possibility that Ireland could be used as a staging point for invasion by Spanish forces seemed to have been eliminated by the planned genocide by starvation of the Irish population in 1600–1,[89] and by the subsequent plantation of English settlers and the economic recovery. Scotland was eliminated as a staging point for invasion by French forces by the conversion of the Scottish nobility to

Protestantism and by the union of the two crowns under James I and VI in 1603. France had been so weakened by the Wars of Religion that it no longer appeared as the menace it once had been under Francis I, and would be again under Louis XIV. Men undoubtedly worried about the progress of the Catholic forces in the Thirty Years War, but the victories of Gustavus Adolphus made a stalemate seem to be the most likely outcome, and after the early 1620s few thought that England was directly threatened. As it turned out, the English Civil War was one of the very few in modern history whose outcome was not powerfully influenced by foreign powers (except Scotland). It was fought in one of the rare periods when the neighbouring states of continental Europe were too preoccupied to intervene.

By the 1630s, therefore, the three great pressures which might have held a congeries of ruling élites together and deterred them from fighting amongst themselves were all of them much less severe than they had been for more than a century, or were to be again for a very long time indeed.

Crisis of confidence

The most important cause, and symptom, of the decay of any government or institution is the loss of prestige and respect among the public at large, and the loss of self-confidence among the leaders themselves in their capacity to rule. Just before he took office, President Nixon was warned by one of his closest advisers that 'the sense of institutions being legitimate – especially the institutions of government – is the glue that holds society together. When it weakens, things come unstuck.'[90] The slow but inexorable erosion of this sense of trust may be observed in every sector of English governmental institutions in the late sixteenth and early seventeenth centuries. The credibility gap, as it is called today, manifested itself earliest in the Church, where the laity, from Queen Elizabeth downwards, conspired to treat the clergy, and especially the bishops, with a contempt unequalled before or since. There is no subsequent historical parallel to the simoniacal bargains with the Crown and the courtiers by which Elizabethan bishops were obliged to alienate the hereditary property of their sees in return for their appointments. There is no previous or subsequent parallel to the Act of 1558, which gave the Crown the power to seize valuable episcopal property in exchange for largely worthless bits and pieces of Crown lands. There is certainly no parallel to the carefully baited sexual trap set by an eminently respectable Yorkshire gentleman, Sir Robert Stapleton, to catch the venerable Archbishop Sandys of York, any more than there is a parallel to the savagery of the Marprelate Tracts in the 1580s, or the scatological and scurrilous anti-episcopal pamphleteering of the 1630s.[91]

So affected were the higher clergy by this climate of opinion that many of the early Elizabethan bishops were willing, even anxious, to surrender their powers and their titles and to become mere superintendents of a Church administered in co-operation with well-to-do and zealous laymen. But Elizabeth, convinced of James's later aphorism, 'No, Bishop, No King', would have none of these reformist suggestions, and so the bishops survived, their powers nominally unimpaired, but their wealth reduced and their prestige in decline. Archbishop Sandys wrote despairingly that 'the ministers of the Word, the messengers of Christ, are esteemed *tamquam excrementa mundi.*'[92] Nor were matters improved by the fact that in the late sixteenth and the early seventeenth centuries the bishops were mostly men of lower-middle-class origin and of restricted outlook and experience. Before the Reformation many had been bright young men who had travelled Europe as ambassadors and had served in high positions at Court, or were sons or relatives of squires and noblemen. But now, commented John Selden acidly, 'they are of a low condition, their education nothing of that way.'[93] They could no longer rely on the respect of the influential laity which once had been inspired by the dignity of their office, by their political and administrative experience, and by their breeding.

Equally damaging to the prospects of the Anglican Church in its early years was the legacy from its pre-Reformation past of a parish clergy which was for a long time incapable of meeting the changing needs of the laity. Moreover, the sharp decline in numbers entering the ministry during the disturbed period from 1540 to 1560 meant that in the first twenty years of its existence the Anglican Church suffered from an acute shortage of manpower of any sort, much less men of the high calibre which was now required. In the diocese of Canterbury in 1560 of 274 documented livings, 107 were without an incumbent, of which 42 were served only by a curate and 65 were left without any spiritual attention whatsoever. In the archdeaconry of Oxford where there had been 371 rectors, vicars and curates in 1526, there were still only 270 as late as 1586.[94]

These conditions were most prolonged in the north, and in 1628 an M.P. could reminisce that 'there were some places in England which were scarce in Christendom, where God was little better known than among the Indians . . . where the prayers of the common people are more like spells and charms than devotions'.[95] Even in the better serviced areas, the giddy religious oscillations of the period 1533–60 coupled with the ferocious persecution of those not agile enough to follow the latest trend in official doctrine had left both people and clergy dazed and frightened. Small wonder that the popular assumption was 'that it is the safest to do in religion as most do' – hardly a belief conducive to great spiritual zeal.[96] It was to combat this apathy that the more dedicated laymen were asking more and more of the clergy.

As emphasis on ritual in the Church service declined, the laity increasingly came to expect the parish clergy to be resident, well-educated, respectable preachers who were morally above reproach. These were standards which the sixteenth-century clergy were unequipped to meet. It was not until very late in the century that numbers became adequate, educational levels improved enormously, and the Anglican clergy began by and large to fulfil most of the new requirements, even if their financial rewards continued to be inadequate. A substantial part of the massive expansion of higher education in the late Elizabethan period was devoted to increasing the numbers and raising the intellectual and moral standards of the parochial clergy. The rise of the parish clergy was as much a feature of the age as the rise of the gentry, provided that it is interpreted principally as a rise in status and standards rather than in income. The late medieval parish priest was little more than a semi-literate dirt-farmer of dubious morals: the Caroline minister of a parish had a university degree, strong religious convictions, a comfortable house, some books on his shelves, and the sheet-anchor of a wife and children to divert him from the immoderate pursuit of wine or women. A late seventeenth-century bishop could plausibly claim that 'in the long reign of Queen Elizabeth and King James, the clergy of the Reformed Church of England grew the most learned of the world.'[97]

This change for the better in the quality of the clergy was supported by the construction by Hooker and others of the intellectual, historical and theological underpinnings which the Church had hitherto lacked. Together they were sufficient to secure the ultimate triumph of Anglicanism at the Restoration. But neither could solve the serious economic problems of the Church and the improvement came too late to prevent the formation of powerful dissenting elements, since many of the most energetic among the new clergy had picked up Puritan sympathies along with their education. Many others were by 1640 almost equally enthusiastic Anglicans, so that the educational and spiritual regeneration of the clergy actually increased religious fragmentation by splitting the ranks of Protestant zealots.

The failure of so many of the Anglican bishops and clergy to match up to the expectations of the laity in the early Elizabethan period led to a search by many conscientious men and women for a more inspiring and convincing religious experience and a more responsive religious organization. A vacuum of religious zeal was created by the non-preaching, non-proselytizing, absentee clergy of the church established by Elizabeth, and it was filled by two groups of dedicated and determined men who differed utterly in their religious loyalties and beliefs, but were very similar in the intensity of their faith and their missionary enthusiasm. The first group was the seminary priests who flooded back into England and built up a wholly new, firmly entrenched, Catholic minority of influential noblemen and gentlemen, together with their servants and tenants.[98] This new Catholic community was constructed on the ashes of the old pre-Reformation church, but it owed far less to a continuity of faith and loyalty than to the absence of a respect-worthy alternative in the Anglican Church, and to the powerful moral force of the missionary priests.

On the other flank arose a group of dedicated Puritan ministers and preachers, many of them Marian exiles. They enjoyed the support of a significant number of influential peers, courtiers and gentry, who were pressing for purification of the Anglican Church from within, and who used their patronage of Church livings and university positions to protect the ministers from official persecution. Elizabeth's obdurate refusal to compromise which this moderately reformist group was the greatest blunder of her career, and one that was to have momentous consequences for English history. Not only did it exacerbate relations with her Parliaments for many years, but it also drove many moderate Puritan reformers to formulate demands for radical changes in church organization. Although she successfully stamped out the Presbyterian movement in her time, Puritanism as a dissident force in the universities and the Church survived unimpaired, under the protection of its numerous and influential lay patrons, and it came to the surface again in 1603 with the Milleniary Petition. Compromise was once more rejected, mainly by the bishops, and the stage was set for a still more violent confrontation after the death of the easy-going James and the retirement of the sympathetic Archbishop Abbott.[99]

The chance of rallying opinion around a unified national church admittedly was not very great in 1558, but, such as it was, it had probably disappeared altogether by 1610. As a result, the Established Church did not even enjoy the loyalty of all its own ministers, at a time when it was trying to fight a war on two fronts with Catholics on the right and sectaries on the left. Nearly all contemporaries doubted whether a state could survive if the religious loyalties of its subjects were divided, and the historical record tends to support them. Lord Burghley, a moderate political pragmatist in religion if ever there was one, thought that 'There could be no government where there was division, and that state could never be in safety where there was toleration of two religions.' His son, the Earl of Salisbury, was equally certain that toleration of open dissenters was 'the highway to break all the bonds of unity, to nourish schism in the Church and Commonwealth'.[100] Archbishop Laud regarded it as impossible that 'the church should melt and the State stand firm', and his sworn enemies in Massachusetts agreed with him in this, if in nothing else. In 1648 Nathaniel Ward, a New England minister, delivered on behalf of the Eastern Association a passionate petition to the House of Commons on the evils of religious pluralism, arguing that a State cannot endure with 'two dissenting forms of church-government in one and the same polity, unless it be a state where religion is but form and policy'. It was for this reason that the conventional seventeenth-century view was that of President Urian Oakes of Harvard, who regarded 'unbounded toleration as the first-born of all abominations'.[101] Until ideological passions subsided in the late seventeenth century, a population that was deeply split on religious issues tended to be extremely difficult to keep at peace. When toleration came, it was not a triumph of moral principle over political expediency, but of political expediency over religious principle. Only when religious enthusiasm ebbed and the enforcement of the ideal of uniformity was recognized as a greater threat to the stability of the political system than the introduction of toleration, did contemporaries reluctantly agree to try to live together within a religiously pluralist community. Toleration is a child of indifference.

If the prestige and power of the Anglican episcopacy were in decline in the early years of Elizabeth, so also, though at a slower pace and at a later stage, were those of the titular aristocracy.[102]

Their military power was the first to go. The gigantic estates of the old medieval magnates were broken up, and with them went control of large numbers of potential soldiers. At the same time loyalties began to shift, the influence of nobles over client gentry and tenantry being weakened by increasing landlord absenteeism, and by the trend towards economic rents which severely reduced the service element in landlord-tenant relations. The noblemen were themselves losing the military capacity either to fight against their sovereign, or to serve him as military leaders in time of war. Devoted to court life, administration, or rural pursuits, they failed to acquire the technical competence and experience needed for military command in a Renaissance war. They were also losing their self-confidence as they found themselves increasingly tied to the royal chariot by chains of hope, fear and duty.

The aristocracy suffered a severe loss of their landed capital in the late Elizabethan period, primarily because of improvident sales made in order to keep up the style of life they considered necessary for the maintenance of status. When they abandoned sales of land and took to rigorous economic exploitation of what was left in order to maximize profits, they certainly restored their financial position, but at the expense of much of the loyalty and affection of their tenants. They salvaged their finances at the cost of their influence and prestige. This was particularly unfortunate since other factors were combining to reduce that influence and prestige. The most important of these was the granting of titles of honour for cash not merit, in too great numbers, and to too unworthy persons, which both lowered respect for the hierarchy of ranks, and infuriated those who lost out in the scramble. As de Tocqueville pointed out with reference to the causes of the French Revolution, the injustice of such a system of upward mobility generates even greater resentment and hatred among the élite than a blocking of mobility channels altogether.

Other causes of the decline in respect for the aristocracy were the under-mining of their electoral influence because of the rise of deeply-felt political and religious issues; their increasing preference for extravagant living in the city instead of hospitable living in the countryside; and growing doubts about their attitudes, real or supposed, toward constitutional theory, the methods and scale of taxation, forms of worship, aesthetic tastes, financial probity and sexual morality. Only Puritan noblemen like the Earl of Bedford and the Earl of Warwick preserved, and possibly even increased, their prestige and political influence.

The third element of the establishment arch, along with the Church and the aristocracy, was the Court, that ever-shifting group (some of them bishops or aristocrats) of advisers, servants, officials, and hangers-on who gathered in ever-increasing numbers about the Renaissance princes of Europe.[103] As local patronage became more and more concentrated in the hands of the Crown, as tax revenues of the state increased, as the bureaucracy expanded, so the Court became not only the monopolistic centre of political power, but also a market place for the disposal of an ever-increasing volume of cash, pensions, jobs, monopolies, and favours of all kinds. The successful operation of the Court system depended on the maintenance of a delicate and extremely complicated political balance, by which no one faction was ever allowed to establish a grip on either the policy-making or the patronage-dispensing mechanism, and in which the favours distributed were sufficiently widespread to satisfy a majority of the influential supplicants, but were not so inordinately lavish as to arouse the indignation of the taxpayers. The Early Stuarts failed on both counts. For eleven years, from 1618 to 1629, they allowed policy and patronage to be placed at the disposal of a single favourite, George Villiers, Duke of Buckingham; for a quarter of a century, from 1603 to 1629, they dissipated royal resources in extravagant gifts and absurdly opulent Court festivities, and they channelled the bulk of their generosity into the hands of a favoured few. This irritated the many powerful nobles and courtiers who were left out in the cold, and it enraged the gentry in the House of Commons, providing them with legitimate grounds for the refusal of any more Parliamentary grants of taxation. This refusal in turn obliged the King to auction off his powers for economic regulation, appointment to office, and the creation of new honours, actions which further heightened political tensions.

In the early and middle years of the reign of Elizabeth, the Court successfully contained within a single political system of multiple checks and balances the representatives of a series of conflicting ideas and interests: Anglicans, and Puritans, magnates and squires, gentlemen and merchants, Court and Country, hawks and doves in foreign and military policy, supporters of the prerogative and supporters of Parliament and the common law, allies and clients on the one hand of the Cecils and on the other of the Dudleys and Devereux. What happened after the rebellion and execution of the Earl of Essex in 1600 was that this central political switchboard broke down, and many of these diverse and increasingly hostile groups began to organize locally and to band together, independently of the national political process at Court and even in open opposition to it.

The growing political alienation of 'Court' from 'Country' was heightened by a parallel cultural and moral alienation, an ideological development which is discussed later on. The composite result was a divorce of sensibility as well as a clash over policy. By the reign of Charles I, the concept of harmony and co-operation within the Commonwealth had almost completely broken down, the two words Court and Country having come to mean political, psychological and moral opposites.

Confidence in and respect for the bureaucracy were declining as fast as they were for the Court and the courtiers. In the first place corruption was growing rapidly at all levels of government, especially the highest.[104] There had inevitably been a great deal of corruption during the hectic years of seizure of Church property and its disposal on the market between 1536 and 1551, but the more efficient administrators, such as Sir William Cecil, had slowly reimposed some sense of order and responsibility.[105] The levels both of corruption itself and of protest against it seem to have subsided between about 1552 and 1588. But in the 1590s the Crown found itself desperately short of money to finance the Anglo-Spanish War, and at the same time advancing age accentuated Elizabeth's temperamental instinct for avarice and meanness. As a result, the flow of favours by which the greater officers of state were normally rewarded was sharply curtailed, at a time when inflation was reducing the fixed fees and salaries of all officials, large and small, to derisory proportions in real terms. The officials were consequently forced into corruption, whether they liked it or not, with the inevitable result of deteriorating public services – the state of the navy in the reign of James is a classic case – and rising public indignation. The last twist to this screw was given by the Duke of Buckingham in the 1620s, as he frankly and cheerfully put everything up for auction, from a bishopric to a judgship to a title of nobility.

The second development which undermined public confidence in the administration was the use made first by Elizabeth and then by the Early Stuarts of their powers for economic regulation, which had been pressed upon the government by an eager Parliament in the second third of the sixteenth century. For the first time in history, men were demanding something more from the State than merely law and order and security against foreign enemies. The rapid

86

economic changes of the period were upsetting old social relationships, and creating new classes of persons who no longer fitted into the old, ordered hierarchical system. There were now very much larger numbers of ruthless entrepreneurs who were disturbing public order by their thrusting materialist drive for economic gain; and there were now very much larger numbers of helpless and dangerous poor who had nowhere to live, and no work by which to support themselves. To deal with these new pressures, the early Tudor humanists, the 'Commonwealthmen' evolved a new concept of the functions of the State, whose duties now included the intelligent exercise of power to curb the excesses that were threatening stability, to increase national wealth, and even to improve the material conditions of all citizens. In response to the rapid pace of social change, law ceased to be the embodiment of custom and tradition, and became an active, working force to mould society. The ideal was still the medieval one of social stability, but the desire to maintain it under changing economic conditions created a wholly new role for the State.[106]

The dilemma of the Tudor monarchy was that public opinion thrust upon it the task of enforcing extensive economic and social regulations without providing it with the administrative powers to carry it out. Parliament passed 'stacks of statutes', controlling many aspects of economic life in the interests of economic self-sufficiency, national defence, stable wage and price levels, quality standards of industrial products, support for the indigent and punishment of the work-shy, and other desirable social objectives.[107] But since there were no paid local officials and inadequate central administrative and legal machinery, the Crown was obliged to resort to the use of professional informers working for profit. These men, who naturally tended to be recruited from the dregs of society, promptly turned to extortion and blackmail as an easier way to maximize profits than by the enforcement of the law.[108] In later years of Elizabeth the Crown, hard pressed for funds to reward its servants, began to use these powers of economic regulation to put money in the pocket of influential courtiers and clients by granting them the proceeds from their exclusive enforcements.[109] What started out as a bold legislative attempt at social engineering ended in a squalid administrative exercise in corrupt exploitation of producers and consumers. The monopolist became a stock figure of evil in the early seventeenth century, and efforts were made by Parliament to curb his activities by the Statute of Monopolies in 1624. But these efforts were in vain, and an important reason for the attack on so many administrative units and powers in 1640–2 was pent-up exasperation at the open perversion of economic controls. Few things aroused more public indignation, few things did more to discredit the administration.

Finally the keystone of the arch, the monarchy itself, fell into disrepute. Henry VIII and Elizabeth had been the foci of an adulation which evidently sprang to some degree from a deep ground-swell of popular nationalist feeling, even if much of it today seems nauseating in its jingo ideology and its sycophantic flattery of the monarch. Both gained enormously from the Divine Right theories of the early Protestant reformers, and the nationalistic conviction of the later Anglicans. It was William Tyndale who pronounced in 1528: 'He that resisteth the King resisteth God . . . The King is, in this world, without law, and may at his lust do right or wrong, and shall give account but to God alone.' No wonder that eight years later Henry VIII was boldly telling his subjects 'I have chief charge of you under God, both of your souls and bodies.' It was the future Bishop Latimer who began to speak of 'the God of England', and it was the future Bishop Aylmer in 1559 who went one stage further and proclaimed that 'God is English'. The theme was taken up by John Lyly in 1580 with his paean of self praise: 'Oh blessed peace, oh happy Prince, oh fortunate people. The living God is only the English God.' This doctrine, which nationalized the Deity and linked Him to Queen Elizabeth, was given tremendous impetus by the widespread diffusion of John Foxe's *Book of Martyrs*, which interpreted the accession of Queen Elizabeth as a final act of God's providence, which saved the true religion for all the peoples of the world.[110]

This association of Queen Elizabeth's person with the sense of national identity was fortified by a carefully orchestrated propaganda campaign in portraiture, ballad, poetry, and prose. Ballads circulated widely with the repeated refrain:

> A most renowned virgin Queen,
> Whose like on earth was never seen.

Poets poured out a never-ending stream of the hyperbolic adulation, stressing Elizabeth's dual role as 'Religion's guardian, Peace's patroness', her function as the unifying figure who preserved England for the Protestant religion, and kept at bay the destructive flames of civil war. In many of the more popular ballads, the adoration of the Virgin Queen was subconsciously serving as a secular substitute for the worship of the Virgin Mary.[111] This extraordinary

campaign certainly did much to assure the stablity of the Elizabethan regime. But the trouble with a personality cult is that it is a
hard act to follow. The iconographic association of Elizabeth's person
with the national destiny had its danger for her successors, since it
tended to blur the distinction between the 'King's Two Bodies',
between the mortal flesh of the current monarch and the immortal
institution of monarchy. The closer became the identification of Elizabeth's person with English religious nationalism, the more difficult it
became to pass the identification on to her successor. It was the
Stuarts who had to pay the political bill for the exaltation of Elizabeth.

If their task was thus difficult to begin with, it was made still more
so by their own personal failings. James had no charisma whatever
and Charles very little; neither were much loved or feared either by
those who were fairly close to them or by the people at large. As a
hated Scot, James was suspect to the English from the beginning,
and his ungainly presence, mumbling speech and dirty ways did not
inspire respect. Reports of his blatantly homosexual attachments
and his alcoholic excesses were diligently spread back to a horrified
countryside. What was the world to make of a King who could write
to a young subject, as James did to the Duke of Buckingham:

> for God so love me, as I desire only to live in this world for
> your sake, and that I had rather live banished in any part of
> the earth with you than live a sorrowful widow's life without
> you. And so God bless you, my sweet child and wife, and grant
> that you may ever be a comfort to your dear dad and husband.
> James R.

In casual conversation about the Duke of Buckingham Sir Walter
Raleigh could remark that royal favourites were 'frequently com-
manded to uncomely, and sometimes unnatural, employments'; a
preacher at the popular May Day sermon at St Paul's Cross openly
referred to the King and 'his catamites'; correspondents from the
Court regaled their friends with detailed accounts of drunken orgies
in which men and women were staggering and spewing around the
King; it was reported that when hunting the King did not dismount
in order to relieve himself, and so habitually ended the day in a filthy
and stinking condition. In the light of these stories it was clear that
the sanctity of monarchy itself would soon be called into question.[112]

Worse still was the fact that James's pro-Spanish foreign policy
and his close association with the Spanish ambassador Gondomar
exposed him to the (wholly unjustified) accusations of popish

sympathies and a betrayal of England's national interests. Nor were these many defects offset by any attempts to seek public acclaim, A shrewd foreign critic noted that 'He does not make much of his subjects, and does not receive them with the same cordiality by which Queen Elizabeth used to gain the hearts of the people. Thus while the Queen acquired the intense love of the people, the present King is hated and despised by them.' It was with these memories in mind that after the Civil War and the fall of the monarchy the Earl of Newcastle advised Charles II that when he regained his throne he should 'show yourself gloriously to your people like a God, as in Queen Elizabeth's time.'[113] Charles I was far more respectable than his father in his personal habits, but he was no more successful in winning popular admiration, and he had a cold, arrogant and yet furtive manner that aroused both hostility and suspicion among those who dealt with him. Worst of all was the fact that his devotion to his Catholic Queen and his employment of Catholic ministers exposed him to serious and widespread suspicions of popery.

By 1640 there was not much left of 'the divinity that doth hedge a King', and the current defenders of the still popular myth of the English as God's Chosen People were now using it as a stick with which to beat King Charles. Preachers of inflammatory sermons before the House of Commons encouraged further intransigence towards the monarch by telling the House that Parliament, not King Charles, was the true heir of Queen Elizabeth, and was now God's chosen instrument to rebuild Zion and overthrow false gods. By 1640 Puritan preachers were calling the House of Commons 'The House of Gods and the House of mortal Gods'. Divine Right had been transferred from Whitehall to Westminster. After war had broken out, the nationalist myth of the English was used to rally the more radical supporters of Parliament, and in 1643 John Milton announced in his magisterial way that 'now that God is decreeing to begin some new and great period in his Church, even to the reforming of Reformation itself, what does He then but reveal himself to his Englishmen; I say, as his manner is, first to us.'[114] The logical result of this new twist given to the old jingo myth was not merely the destruction of the perverted Anglican Church but also the execution of the King as the arch-practitioner of ungodly – and thus unEnglish – activities. There is about the stately ceremony of the royal execution in Whitehall more than a hint of the ritual murder of the priest-king, in expiation for the sins of the tribe and to cleanse the land of the evils which had befallen it.

Although the finest flower of the Divine Right of Kings theory, Robert Filmer's *Patriarcha*, only achieved popularity and influence after the Restoration, it seems to have been more a last-ditch effort to prop up a crumbling institution than a symptom of triumphant ideological resurgence. After the Restoration the clergy and the Tory gentry spoke incessantly of their devotion to the principles of Divine Right and Non-Resistance to a lawful king, but the very stridency of their professions betrays an inner insecurity. In 1688 they were faced with the unpleasant reality of a Catholic king and a Catholic heir to the throne. In these circumstances they abandoned all these notions with a suddenness which suggests that, beneath all the sound and fury, the concept of divinely inspired and ordained monarchy had been dealt an all but irreparable blow by the events of the first half of the century.

This erosion of confidence in and respect for so many elements of authority in both Church and State was greatly aided by the weekly distribution throughout the country of knowledgeable, detailed and malicious gossip about the London scene by a handful of 'intelligencers', the first professional journalists. Spiced with lurid stories about the sexual scandals at the Court, and about the financial scandals in the administration, these letters sent out regularly from London, together with the libels and obscene poems which also had wide circulation in manuscript, were a powerful influence in undermining public confidence in government. 'Then were the seeds of future sedition sown, with an evil report on David's government, that all the people might loath it and after rise up to pluck it down' observed a Royalist cleric after the Restoration, and the Duke of Newcastle advised Charles II to be sure to suppress the letter-writers and libellers when he got his throne back.[115]

Rise of the opposition

The counterpart to the decay of government was the rise of opposition as a self-conscious political force. It was in Parliament, and particularly in the House of Commons, that the opposition built its institutional base. An important reason why this national representative body continued to play so important a role in English political life is that, unlike the provinces in France, the administrative subdivisions, the counties, had always been too small to serve as foci for political activity, except on a very limited scale. As a result the central representative institution had no serious rivals and gained steadily in prestige and power, until men actually fought and even paid to be members of it, instead of having to be paid their expenses as an inducement to serve. With its control over taxation, especially for war, and its control over legislation, especially concerning religion, it was strategically placed to demand redress of grievances. During the course of the middle and late sixteenth century many things happened to increase Parliament's powers and to diminish the capacity of the Crown to control it. The House of Commons grew from about 300 to about 500, and the gentry component in it rose from about 50 per cent to about 75 per cent, despite the fact that most new seats were borough seats.[116] The members gained experience and a sense of continuity owing to the enhanced frequency of Parliamentary sessions between 1590 and 1614. They developed an efficient committee system, which freed them from manipulation by a Crown-appointed Speaker, and by the early seventeenth century Parliamentary leaders were beginning to emerge, men who built their careers on playing a key role in debates and on committees of the House. The Crown had serious trouble with this body at all times in the late sixteenth and early seventeenth centuries but slowly the nature of the trouble changed and became far more menacing. In the early years of Elizabeth's reign, there were quarrels over specific issues – religion or taxation or foreign policy – but by the early seventeenth century there is visible the beginning of a formal opposition, men who came up to Parliament with a set determination to challenge the Crown on a wide range of issues. Loosely calling themselves 'the Patriots' or 'the Country', they developed their own distinct ideology and tactics.[117]

Constitutional issues tend to arise in the first instance from dissatisfaction over specific issues of policy, rather than from a theoretical concern with the distribution of authority. So long as most men are content with official actions, the insoluble question of sovereignty lies dormant. But as soon as government policy is challenged by influential groups of citizens, the question inevitably arises: to what extent are the citizens free to express their views, and what weight are these views to play in the decision-making process? Throughout the reigns of Elizabeth and James I one can observe a growing awareness of just such theoretical questions arising from specific grievances. Dissatisfaction with Elizabeth's refusal to modify her religious policy in a more Puritan direction, her refusal to marry or to settle the succession, her cautious and ambiguous foreign policy, and finally her obstinate defence of a morally untenable position about economic monopolies, slowly drove the more active members of the House of Commons to make wholly new constitutional claims. They moved from a position of asking to speak their minds on issues put before them without fear of punishment, to a position of demanding the right to initiate discussion and influence policy on any issue they chose. First formulated by the radicals in the latter years of Elizabeth's reign, this demand became increasingly insistent under James as dissatisfaction mounted with his financial ineptitude and his pro-Spanish foreign policy. To concede that the demand for redress of grievances precede the supply of funds, would have given Parliament a whip-hand over the policies of any government which could not live off its hereditary revenues. Because of this, the government was obliged either to change its policies, or to turn to further non-parliamentary ways of raising money. These in turn immediately raised new constitutional questions about their legality. Although the Commons bolstered their case with precedents dredged up from the past, thanks to the antiquarian researches of the common lawyer, in fact the constitutional demands were clearly innovatory and aggressive. The winning òf the initiative by the House of Commons was a radical step achieved under the smokescreen of the conservative ideology of a return to the past.

Constitutional quarrels are far less easy to settle by the normal process of arbitration and compromise than are disputes over specific policies, which by the nature of things tend to have a relatively short life. And so by the 1620s the quarrels of the Crown and the House of Commons had moved from the concrete issues of the royal succession or a modification of the prayer book in the 1560s, to fundamental questions of the right to impeach royal ministers, freedom of speech, consent to taxation and freedom from arbitrary arrest. Once these questions were raised in the theoretical form of issues of principle, they became important motives for action in their own right, driving men to take stands regardless of the particular cases to which they momentarily applied. Most parties continued to pay lip-service to the ideals of the 'balanced constitution', the 'ancient law', the sovereignty of 'King in Parliament'. But such slogans could no longer act as a common bond, since agreement on their interpretation had broken down. Once that agreement had disappeared there naturally arose radicals on either flank whose solution took the form of massive enhancement of the traditional powers of the royal prerogative, or an equally massive shift to control and direction by Parliament.

The constitutional crisis, the mile-stones of which were the Apology of the House of Commons of 1604, Bate's Case of 1606, the revival of impeachment of royal ministers in 1621, the Five Knights' Case in 1627, the Petition of Right in 1628 and the Ship Money Case in 1636, thus arose out of a combination of particular circumstances. On the one hand the classes represented in the House of Commons were becoming increasingly self-confident and self-assertive and were developing technical means of shaking off royal control of their proceedings. On the other the Crown – both Elizabeth and the Early Stuarts – was failing to modify its religious policy, foreign policy, or fiscal policy to take account of the susceptibilities and views of significant elements of the propertied classes, who found spokesmen in many members of Parliament and an influential group of dissidents in the House of Lords.

Too much should not be made of James's theorizing about the Divine Right of Kings, since his bark was worse than his bite, and no sensible man could take his claims too seriously. In any case his views, although more extravagantly phrased and more insistently repeated, did not differ in any significant respect from those of Queen Elizabeth. It was the latter who in 1585 had publicly declared that 'Kings and Princes Sovereigns, owing their homage and service only unto the Almighty God the King of all Kings, are in that respect not bound to yield account or render the reasons of their actions to any other but to God their only Sovereign Lord.' When James explained to Parliament in 1609 that 'Kings are not only God's Lieutenants on earth and sit upon God's throne, but even by God Himself they are called gods', he was raising the level of the rhetoric but hardly altering the basic philosophy.[118] The growing quarrel between the King and the Parliamentary gentry was converted into a constitutional crisis by more serious matters than the rhodomontades of King James. The House of Commons was at odds with the Crown on many issues long before he spoke, and it merely used the injudicious and tactless royal words as a handy stick with which to beat the King.

The conversion of a political crisis into a constitutional crisis did not begin in earnest until 1621, but for the next eight years the Commons moved with remarkable speed to change the constitutional balance. They were exasperated with a pro-Catholic foreign policy, a hopelessly inept military policy, chaotic public finances, and the limitless corruption and nepotism and the overwhelming monopoly of patronage exercised by the Duke of Buckingham. As a result the opposition in Parliament was driven to make unprecedented claims for a share in executive power. James and Charles had reason to be alarmed by the swift erosion of their authority, but the sense of insecurity of the latter led him into extreme courses which only succeeded in alienating his more moderate potential supporters.

At the same time that the gentry in their capacity as M.P.s were beginning to assert themselves and demand a greater share in political decision-making, the same persons, in their role as Justices of the Peace, were gaining increased experience in local administration. In response to the growing burden of enforcing legislation about social control and social welfare, there was a striking increase in their numbers and their experience, and consequently in their power to paralyse the workings of any government of which they seriously disapproved. Little by little the Quarter Sessions of the county developed into a kind of local parliament with the political function of voicing popular grievances; little by little the loyalties of the lesser gentry became increasingly focused on the county, the arena within whose confines they married, quarrelled, intrigued and played politics. Although the élite of rich squires had a wider experience of Europe on the Grand Tour, and of Westminster in Parliament, the horizons of the parish gentry were almost entirely limited to the county.[119]

An important cause of the growing self-confidence of the gentry was the striking improvement of their education. The period saw a very large increase in enrolments in grammar schools, universities, and Inns of Court, in large part caused by the desire of the propertied classes to train their sons for their new responsibilities. In terms of formal attendance of its members at an institution of higher learning, the House of Commons of 1640 was the best-educated in English history before or since. Moreover many, both of the gentry and their electorate were being educated at grammar schools, private schools, and colleges which were staffed by ideological dissidents. The influence on the young Oliver Cromwell of Thomas Beard, his Puritan schoolmaster at the Huntingdon Free School, is only a better known instance of what was happening in hundreds and thousands of cases across the country. Moreover at both universities there were powerful and dedicated Puritan dons whose sermons and conversation must have made an indelible impression upon their pupils. The general tone of Oxford and Cambridge was probably mainly conformist, but there were enough Puritan colleges, or Puritan dons lurking in Anglican colleges, to leaven the whole and to mould the opinions of substantial numbers of future gentry. Acting in their capacities as Chancellors of the respective universities, the broad tolerance exercised by Lord Burghley at Cambridge, and the active encouragement to Puritans provided by the Earl of Leicester at Oxford, did much to sap the foundations of the Established Church before it had time to take root. Even today, it is by no means certain how long a State can survive, if its educational system is largely in the hands of men who reject the values upon which it is based.

Hobbes thought that the actual content of a classical education was itself subversive, quite apart from the dangerous religious ideas to be picked up at schools and universities: 'men ... became acquainted with the democratical principles of Aristotle and Cicero, and from the love of their eloquence fell in love with their politics, and that more and more, till it grew into the rebellion.' At other times and in other places men have studied the classics without drawing such radical conclusions, so that either Hobbes's suggestions were unfounded, or subsequent familiarity has bred indifference, much as it has done to the radical message of the New Testament. But Hobbes was right – though for the wrong reasons – when he claimed that 'The Universities have been to this nation, as the wooden horse to the Trojans.'[120] The universities were turning out an educated clergy and laity in excess of suitable job opportunities, and were thus creating a large and influential group of discontented 'Outs'. Many of these men had acquired a veneration for the common law, had been given strong Puritan leanings, and had been taught by Ramist logic to think for themselves: they could not easily accept the dictates of Kings and bishops.

Meanwhile the electorate of yeomen, freeholders, and shop-keepers was being exposed to an elementary education which at least taught it to read, and particularly to read the Bible. It has been argued in the light of the experience of the twentieth century that the combination of factors most likely to lead to revolution is 'rapid increase in the proportion of the population receiving primary education, but a slow rate of percentage change in gross domestic product *per capita*'.[121] But this presupposes a situation in which there is a normal expectation of an improvement of standards of living, which was hardly the case in the seventeenth century. The expansion of literacy was in fact dangerous in another way, because it aroused expectations of political and religious participation and exposed large numbers of humble people to the heady egalitarian wine of the New Testament.

Literacy and Puritanism went hand in hand, and the whole Leveller movement, fuelled as it was by pamphlet literature, was only possible because remarkably large numbers of the poor in south-eastern England could now read. If one combines the expansion of higher education with the parallel expansion of secondary education in Latin grammar and of elementary literacy, it looks more and more as if this educational explosion was a necessary – but of course not a sufficient – cause for the peculiar and ultimately radical course the revolution took.

At the same time that the members of the House of Commons were flexing their muscles in wrestling with the Crown, friction was developing between legal officials and judges in the various courts of law. In the 1590s there began a bitter struggle over jurisdictions, fees and litigants between the officials of the two old common law courts and their upstart rivals. These rivals were the ecclesiastical courts and the Admiralty Court, both staffed by civil lawyers, the prerogative courts like the Councils of Wales and the North and the Court of Requests, and the unwieldy giant of the Court of Chancery. The battle aligned common lawyers against the civil lawyers but it also tended to split the former down the middle. Most of them were content to pursue their professional careers, which would normally culminate in a judgeship or an office in one of the court bureaucracies. They were willing enough to engage in guerilla warfare with rival courts for prestige and patronage and fees, though not at the cost of open conflict with the Crown, upon whom their promotion depended. But many of them were slowly driven into a position of opposition, partly by the vigorous royal defence of the rival courts and partly by the tactless royal claims to override the basic tenets of the law. Although the judges and officials continued in the main to side with the King – the Crown never lost a constitutional test-case in the courts – many of the practising barristers in the two common law courts increasingly found that their professional interests and inclinations drew them to support the politics of the country party in the House of Commons, and also of the Puritan enemies of the ecclesiastical courts. Many came to the conclusion that they would best advance their professional interests by supporting the political opposition, an alignment which was also congruent with political attitudes concerning the sanctity of property and the ultimate supremacy of the law which they obtained from their training at the Inns of Court.

The chronology of this development centres on the career of Sir

Edward Coke. The interference by the common law judges in the jurisdiction of the rival courts became much more acute with the elevation of Coke to the office of Chief Justice in 1606, a position which he used as a platform from which to increase the range and intensity of the bombardment. Partly because the civil lawyers like John Cowell, the author of *The Interpreter*, were some of the more enthusiastic supporters of royal pretensions, and partly because the threatened courts were valuable institutions for the maintenance of strong administrative and legal order, the Crown felt itself obliged to rally to the support of the prerogative courts, as a result of which the quarrel gradually turned into a legal attack on the powers of the prerogative itself. Things came to a head in 1616 when Coke's truculent intransigence and his wilful obstruction of Chancery and High Commission led to his dismissal. Five years later Sir Edward turned up in the House of Commons as the leader of the 'Country' opposition to royal policies, and the alliance between lawyers and gentry and Puritans was temporarily sealed.[122] The internal legal quarrel had become absorbed into the wider political conflict. Even before this had occurred, the friction over issues of jurisdiction generated between the local authorities of the area and the two regional Councils of Wales and the North had done much to solidify the alliance of gentry and common lawyers against these institutions. The lawyers, and especially the common law judges, were very conservative persons with no real quarrel with the Crown, and had been mainly concerned in the first instance with pursuing a private vendetta against their legal colleagues. But they were a dangerous group to antagonize, and the marriage of convenience between many common lawyers and opposition gentry was one which a wiser government would have tried very hard to avoid.

New ideas and values

A true revolution needs ideas to fuel it – without them there is only a rebellion or a *coup d'état* – and the intellectual and ideological underpinnings of the opposition to the government are therefore of the first importance. Some of these intellectual currents, like devotion to the common law, were very old but became more widespread, while others, like Puritanism or 'Country' ideology, were relatively new; some like Puritanism and legalism, created polarities, while others, like scepticism, were vaguely corrosive of belief. But all helped to undermine confidence in the central institutions of Church and State and there is therefore little need to emphasize any further the undoubted differences in their origins and character.

The most far-reaching in its influence on men's minds, although very difficult to pin down in precise detail, was Puritanism, here interpreted to mean no more than a generalized conviction of the need for independent judgment based on conscience and bible reading. The quintessential quality of a Puritan was not the acceptance of any given body of doctrine, but a driving enthusiasm for moral improvement in every aspect of life, 'a holy violence in the performing of all duties', as Richard Sibbes put it.[123] In practice this zeal found expression in a desire to simplify the services of the Church and to improve the quality of its ministers, to reduce clerical authority and wealth, and, most significant of all, to apply the strictest principles of a particular morality to Church, society and State. These attitudes were held by some nobles, many influential gentry, some big merchants, and very many small tradesmen, artisans, shopkeepers and yeomen. The sociological roots of Puritanism are still obscure, but in England, as elsewhere, there was some correlation between cloth-working and religious radicalism. The spread of Puritanism among the lower middle class may therefore be related to the unusual size of England's prime industrial activity.[124] Other groups which seem peculiarly susceptible to radical religious influences are artisans in sedentary trades in which conversation is a natural accompaniment to work: tailors and shoemakers are cases in point. Among these lower classes the key agents of diffusion were the printed Bible and the spoken sermon, which between them carried the message to thousands of newly literate men and women with an insatiable appetite for moral and religious instruction.

At the level of the gentry and nobility, economic explanations of religious opinions carry no conviction. Social explanations are little better, since there was always tension between the acceptance of existing gradations of rank and privilege and the potentially socially disruptive idea of a hierarchy of the godly. But the landed élite was desperately seeking some new moral justification for its privileged existence, to replace the chivalric ideal of a warrior aristocracy, and the ideal of public service in administration was sanctified by the Puritan concept of the calling. It the gentry could only convince themselves and others that they were also the godly, their position was secure. Secondly, Puritan ideology, by its resolutely anti-popish stand and its glorification of the English as a chosen people, became identified with a rising tide of nationalism which was enormously heightened by the long-lived menace of a Spanish invasion. Third, Puritan hostility to the bishops struck the popular Erastian chord of anti-clericalism and the insistence on lay control over the Church. The potential conflict between the ambitions of Presbyterian ministers and the authority of lay patrons was always present in the English Puritan movement, but it did not come into the open until the hour of victory, in the 1640s. As with the lower classes, the Bible and sermons were the media for the transmission of ideas, but education in the universities, studying the works of Calvin and Beza under the direction of Puritan dons, was undoubtedly a most important, perhaps a critically important, factor.

The political consequences of Puritanism are less difficult to discover than its causes. It provided an essential element in the Revolution, the feeling of certainty in the rectitude of the opposition cause, and of moral indignation at the wickedness of the established authorities. It also helped to construct the theoretical justification for a challenge to the existing order. What if the Elect of God are not identical with the political leaders of the State? What if the Anglican church is not part of the Covenant? Are there limits to the obedience a godly person owes to a sinful magistrate? These were questions to which there were no easy answers, and Puritans of varying stripes wrestled with them for over half a century before coming to a final resolute, conclusion that resistance was both legitimate and necessary. It can plausibly be argued that the mere posing of the questions was ultimately subversive, as their opponents always claimed, since the legitimacy of authority depends upon its unquestioning, thoughtless acceptance. When Cartwright argued that the lay power should exercise its authority 'according to the rules of God', Whitgift was quick to point out that his words could be construed to 'contain the overthrow of the Prince's authority in ecclesiastical and civil matters'. This was a dilemma which socially and politically conservative Puritans – and they were legion – were incapable of solving. When Bancroft asked what would happen 'if Gospel should wrest the sword out of any civil magistrate's hand', they had no ready answer.[125]

It is not easy for a government to deal with men who begin their wills with the calm assurance of moral superiority of a Sir Francis Hastings in 1596: 'Almighty God . . . in his foreknowledge, and before I was put to work either good or evil, hath chosen me to be his child, and predestined me to eternal salvation.' Men with such convictions are stubborn and self-righteous, and do not bend easily to the dictates of authority. Bishop Aylmer was right when he claimed that Puritanism inevitably led to 'greater boldness of the meaner sort', and Matthew Brooks, Master of Trinity College, Cambridge, was partly right when he told Archbishop Abbott in 1630 that 'This doctrine of predestination is the root of puritanism, and puritanism is the root of all rebellions and disobedient untractableness in Parliament, etc., and of all schism and sauciness in the country, nay in the church itself.'[126] Like all authoritarian personalities, the Laudians could not abide 'sauciness' above all things, and this, they realized at last, was where predestination led. The adoption of Arminian theology had political and social implications that were crystal clear to contemporaries, which was why Charles I threw his full influence behind the Arminian clergy.

This independence of moral judgment about the religious and political hierarchy, and later the development of sectarian pluralism, arose from the process of individual interpretation of the vernacular Bible, the free access to which was regarded by Hobbes as one of the principal causes of the Revolution. He complained that 'after the Bible was translated into English, every man, nay every boy and wench, that could read English thought they spoke with God Almighty and understood what He said.'[127]

Equally subversive of passive acceptance of the *status quo* and of obedience to the established authorities in Church and State was the element of chiliasm which lurked in so many Puritan breasts.[128] Puritans may have been conservative in most of their ideas, but their eager anticipation of the creation of a City upon a Hill, a New Jerusalem, could be a powerful stimulus to radical change. For a long time the Puritan laity had looked hopefully to the Prince, the magistrates and the bishops to take the necessary steps to bring about the millenium on earth, but by 1641 they had given up on the established authorities, and had turned to the radical ministers for guidance, as the sermons delivered before the House of Commons show. Without absolute confidence in the rectitude of their cause, which nothing other than Puritanism could have given, the Parliamentary leaders of the 1640s would have been unable to bring themselves to the pitch of defying the King and levying war against him. Their actions flew in the face of a century of propaganda about the sanctity of monarchy and the absolute necessity of obedience to authority as the only protection from anarchy. The extraordinary strength of this tradition is best seen in the last speeches on the scaffold of unsuccessful Tudor rebels, all of whom without exception acknowledged the wickedness of their actions. Not one had the assurance to make a bold statement of defiance before he laid his head on the block.[129] But this assurance was in the end provided by Puritanism, as it slowly became apparent that it was vain any longer to 'tarry for the magistrate'. If the sovereign was no longer the living embodiment of the divine will for the sanctified English people – as Elizabeth, for all her faults, had clearly been – then who was to take on the role? Slowly there occurred a transfer of values from the now incorrigibly evil and papistically inclined King and Court, to the godly magistrates on the benches of the House of Commons and at the Quarter Sessions in the country towns. Once the transfer was complete, as it was in many eyes by 1640, there had been created the will to resist the Crown to the end.

It should be emphasized however, that much of the ultimately subversive character of Puritanism came about by accident rather than design. It crept in through the back door of the many programmes and policies the Puritans were advocating, usually without their knowledge or consent. Almost without exception, they believed strongly in the preservation of the traditional social and political hierarchies and in the preservation of traditional values. But the results of their activities did not work out this way. Although on the one hand their Covenant theology tended to strengthen legalism and contractual obligation, on the other their emphasis on conscience tended in the other direction. By stressing the superiority of individual conscience and biblical interpretation over the dictates of the law, they threw doubts upon the legitimacy of parts of the legal system, particularly the Church courts and the High Commission. They believed in clerical leadership, but their stress on the importance of the personal worth of the priest was a powerful factor in undermining respect for the ordained ministry as a separate caste with special powers. They attacked the legitimacy of the bishops with no thought of attacking other institutions of social order. But both Elizabeth and the Stuarts regarded the abolition of episcopacy as but the prelude to the abolition of hierarchy in society. This may in part have become a self-fulfilling prophecy through the unwise association of monarchy with episcopacy, but the events of the 1640s suggests that the Crown had some truth on its side. Few Puritans favoured participatory democracy for its own sake, but their actions certainly encouraged it. Puritan insistence on popular literacy in order to be able to read the Scriptures, and on popular preaching in order to be able to interpret them correctly, ended up by politicizing the yeomen and urban artisans. The result was the torrent of mass petitioning, the frequent mob actions and the emergence of the Leveller movement, which characterized the 1640s. This was an outcome which was very far from the minds of the Puritan preachers of the previous half-century.

Apart from the working of these accidentally subversive ideas, the second major contribution of the Puritans was to provide an embryo organization out of which grew true radicalism. The Presbyterian *classes* of the 1570s, and the congregations clustering around the Puritan lecturers in the urban churches of the 1620s and 1630s, were the models for ideological party organization. Like Communist Party cells in the twentieth century, they were organized in exclusive units of dedicated enthusiasts under the leadership of an élite. They practised guided democracy with wide participation in discussion combined with firm direction from above, and rigid discipline in the execution of policy. After the Restoration, Bishop Hacket was convinced that 'Conventicles in Corporations were the seminaries out of which the warriors against King and Church came.'[130]

Finally, Puritanism provided the opposition with the necessary leadership. The Puritan lobby in the House of Commons in the days of Elizabeth has been described as the first political party in English history, and the Puritan ministers played a decisive part as propagandists and links which bound the various opposition elements together.[131] For it was not only ideas and moral conviction that Puritanism offered, it was also direction and planning. Puritans were the clerical and secular leaders of the opposition, in and out of Parliament, to Elizabeth's religious and foreign policies. They mounted the propaganda drive via the lectureships in the towns, they led the attack on Buckingham's character and policies in the 1620s. It was through their associations, first as Feoffees for Impropriations and then as directors of the Providence Island Company, that their leaders could assemble in private to lay the plans for the overthrow of Charles's government in the 1630s.[132] It is as safe as any broad generalization of history can be to say that without the ideas, the organization and the leadership supplied by Puritanism there would have been no revolution at all.

The second intellectual basis of the Revolution was the common law.[133] It is noticeable how much of the debates in Parliament in the early seventeenth century was conducted in terms of law and with reference to legal precedents. The great constitutional issues of the day were fought out in test case after test case – Bates' Case, Five Knights' Case, Ship Money Case – and it was only when the opposition had lost them all that it took to radical legislation to change the legal ground rules. This intensive legalism was as pervasive as Puritanism in its effect on the mental set of the early seventeenth century. Increasing numbers of gentry rounded off their education by two or three years at the Inns of Court, where they read some law and rubbed shoulders and ate meals with actual and prospective barristers and judges.[134] Even after this short period of fairly intimate exposure to the law and its practitioners had come to an end, a gentleman was still involved in legal affairs, whether he liked it or not, thanks to the maze of litigation in which every man of property was entangled. The experience may or may not have increased his affection and respect for the legal profession, but it certainly improved his knowledge of the law, a knowledge that he continued to use and respect in his capacity as Justice of the Peace.

From the middle ages the lawyers had inherited a set of rules and conventions which they could, and eventually did, use to erect barriers for the protection of private property, private interests, and private persons against the encroachment of a centralizing state. These defences were based on the medieval concept of liberties, of private vested interests, but they were not the less effective for that. From those particular positions, there emerged a broader ideology of the common law. Sir Edward Coke and others developed a whole field of antiquarian research which they used to buttress the concept of the balanced constitution, using – or abusing – the myth of Magna Carta as the foundation stone. James I remarked that 'ever since his coming to the Crown the popular sort of lawyers have been the men that most affrontedly in all Parliaments have trodden upon his Prerogative.'[135] The lawyers' belief in the immense antiquity of the common law encouraged belief in the existence of an ancient constitution which predated, and was somehow immune from, the royal prerogative. By the 1620s they were looking to Parliament as the guardian of this constitution. It is no coincidence that the main achievement of the Long Parliament in its first year of existence was the abolition of the prerogative courts, which were both the new supports of royal power and the old rivals of the common law courts. This was the one issue upon which gentry, Puritans and lawyers were united.

Although it has been argued earlier that the basis of the quarrel between the common law courts and the prerogative courts began as a struggle over jurisdictions and the fees of litigants, it is none the less true that by the time the quarrel took on a political character, the ideology of the common law had become a powerful independent force. The use made by the opposition of medieval precedents culled from the records in Sir Robert Cotton's library, so conveniently situated close to the House of Commons, was not merely a matter of the cynical manipulation of inapposite precedents for current political purposes. The pedantic legal antiquaries like Hakewill and Coke and Prynne believed deeply in the principles they dredged out of the past, however self-serving their attitudes may seem to historians of a later age. The sanctity of individual property rights was to them, as it was to Ireton and to Locke after them, the keystone of the arch of government, and it was these rights which the Stuart monarchy seemed to be violating, first in its desperate search for ways to tax the rich, and then in its determination to subordinate private interests to the public good. The fact that the common lawyers stood to gain financially from the defence of individual rights of property should not blind us to the depth and sincerity of their convictions on these issues. Most of them were self-deceivers rather than cynics.

The third component in the mentality of the opposition was the ideology of the 'Country'. Spread by poets and preachers, and stimulated by the news letters about the goings-on at Court, it defined itself most clearly as the antithesis to this negative reference group.[136] The Country is firstly an ideal. It is that vision of rustic arcadia that goes back to the Roman classics and which fell on the highly receptive ears of the newly educated gentlemen of England who had studied Virgil's *Georgics* at Oxford or Cambridge.[137] It was a vision of environmental superiority over the City: the Country was peaceful and clean, a place of grass and trees and birds, the City was ugly and dirty and noisy, a place of clattering carts and coaches, coal dust and smog, and piles of human excrement. It was also a vision of moral superiority over the Court; the Country was virtuous, the Court wicked; the Country was thrifty, the Court extravagant; the Country was honest, the Court corrupt; the Country was chaste and heterosexual, the Court promiscuous and homosexual; the Country was sober, the Court drunken; the Country was nationalist, the Court xenophile; the Country was healthy, the Court diseased; the Country was outspoken, the Court sycophantic; the Country was the defender of old ways and old liberties, the Court the promoter of administrative novelties and new tyrannical practices; the Country was solidly

Protestant, even Puritan, the Court was deeply tainted by popish leanings.

Secondly, the Country is a culture and a style of life, again defined as much by what it is not as by what it is. As its name implies, it stood for rural residence in a country house, as opposed to living in rented lodgings in London; for the assumption by the owner of paternalist and patriarchal responsibilities as employer of domestic labour, dispenser of charity, landlord of tenants, and member of the bench of justices. All this was contrasted with the egocentric, hedonist, carefree existence of the man-about-town. The Country also stood for an experience of the world confined to the shires of England, as opposed to the sophistication bred of the Grand Tour through France and Italy; for the maintenance of open hospitality for all, as opposed to the offering of luxurious private dinner parties in the City; for a highly conservative taste in Jacobethan architecture, as opposed to the new-fangled classicism of Inigo Jones; for a highly conservative taste in portrait-painting, as opposed to the courtly continental innovations of Van Dyke; for a highly conservative taste in clothes, as opposed to the dizzily changing fashions of the *beau monde* at Court. By the early seventeenth century England was experiencing all the tensions created by the development within a single society of two distinct cultures, cultures that were reflected in ideals, religion, art, literature, the theatre, dress, deportment and way of life.

Third, the Country is a place, and an institutional structure associated with it. When an Englishman in the early seventeenth century said, 'my country' he meant 'my county'. What we see in the half century before the civil war is the growth of an emotional sense of loyalty to the local community, and also of institutional arrangements to give that sentiment force. The county evolved as a coherent political and social community, with reference to – and potentially in rivalry with – both other counties and the central executive and its local agents such as the Councils of Wales and the North. In the fifteenth and early sixteenth centuries the gentry had been attached to the families of great magnates, both by upbringing in their households and by the subsequent political bonds of 'good lordship'. These were ties which cut across county lines and split counties into fragments. But the decline of the magnate household as an educational centre and its replacement by school and university, and the decline of the ties of 'good lordship' to local noblemen, freed the gentry for a realignment of their loyalties. One focus was the county, organized around the bench of justices. The increase in the numbers of resident gentry in the countryside, their habit of marrying with other families within the county, the growing burden of administrative business thrown by the government on the shoulders of the J.P.s, the increase in number and professional efficiency of the bench, all stimulated the emergence of the Quarter Sessions as a sort of local parliament in which the leading men of the county met at intervals to do business and also to express their sense of county solidarity by the formulation of 'Country' grievances against the Court.

But the country gentry did not only feel loyalty and affection towards particularist local interests and institutions, for the paradox of English history is that up to the nineteenth century central and local loyalties and powers grew together and in parallel. Besides devotion to the Country, the other focus of the loyalty of a gentle-man was the nation, shown by an increased sense of national iden-tity and an increased respect for its head, the Tudor monarchy, and for its representative institution, Parliament. The most presti-gious position a country gentleman could hold was therefore that of knight of the shire, the representative of his county at Westminster. The alienation of the gentry from the early Stuart kings was a product of frustrated idealism, as the later Tory Royalism shows, and their devotion to Parliament is proved by their struggles to win election to it, and their anger over the rough treatment it received. What they wanted, therefore, was to redefine the relationship between central authority and local authority, between Court and Country, so as to bring the two once more into harmonious and balanced relationship. The fourth aspect of the 'Country' is thus a national political programme.

This programme did not alter much throughout the seventeenth century, and was based on a clear, if not very practical, definition of roles and functions. The political theory to which the Country subscribed was one which idealized the so-called 'ancient constitu-tion', which consisted of an equilibrium of governmental organs in which Parliament's function was not to exercise or share power with the executive, but merely to place checks on the exorbitant use of that power.

Society is made up of a court and a country; government of court and Parliament; Parliament of Court and Country members. The court is the administration. The country consists

of men of property; all others are servants. The business of
Parliament is to preserve the independence of property, on
which is founded all human liberty and all human excellence.
The business of government is to govern, and that is a
legitimate authority; but to govern is to wield power, and
power has a natural tendency to encroach. It is more
important to supervise government than to support it, because
the preservation of independence is the ultimate political good.[138]

When the gentry met, not as J.P.s in Quarter Sessions in the county
town but in their alternative capacity as members of Parliament at
Westminster, they increasingly came to look upon themselves as
representatives of the property-owning constituents they left behind
them, and to see their objective as the implementation of the theory
described. To be specific, the Country wanted local offices left in
local hands, the removal of economic controls exercised by the
central government, the end of interference by bishops in local lay
patronage in the Church, some restriction on the taxing powers of
the central government, the abolition of regional courts like those of
Wales and the North, a reduction in expenditure on the Court, and
also a throughly Protestant – but inexpensive – foreign policy.

It is important to realize that the conflict between loyalty to the
particularist locality and loyalty to the nation was fought out within
the mind of each individual gentleman. Moreover many gentry were
also powerfully influenced by other ideas only incidentally related to
the Country ideology, like Puritanism and legalism. It is consequently too simple to attempt to make the Court/Country antithesis the
sole organizing principle around which to build an explanation of
the outbreak of civil war. In any case the antithesis is only one version
of the normal state of tension that exists in all organized societies
between the centralizing and the decentralizing forces: between
Hamilton and Jefferson, for example. Since the polarity continued
to play an important political role in England at least for another
seventy-five years after 1640, it cannot be regarded as the exclusive
cause for a breakdown of government. This is especially so since,
when the crisis came, the lines of division did not run with mathematical precision between the country gentry and the courtiers. Many
gentry saw the virtues of strong monarchical rule, and not a few
courtiers fell off the bandwagon when it began to totter.

The last and most difficult intellectual movement to handle, or
even to document, is the spread of scepticism, which was slowly

eroding belief in traditional values and traditional hierarchies. The new scientific attitudes and discoveries, of which Bacon was so strenuous a promoter, were important less in themselves than for what they did to shatter old certainties. Once it was discovered that the earth was not the centre of the solar system, it immediately became questionable whether man was God's choice creation. As Donne put it in a much quoted passage:[139]

> And new philosophy calls all in doubt . . .
> 'Tis all in pieces, all coherence gone,
> All just supply and all relation.
> Prince, Subject, Father, Son are things forgot.

The last line holds the key to this passage, with its suggestion of the linked collapse of old authority patterns in both the State and the family. Attempts to show a direct association between Baconian optimism about the potentialities of scientific innovation on the one hand and political radicalism during the revolution on the other have not been very convincing.[140] It is possible to detect a renewal of interest in Baconianism during the Interregnum, and there is no doubt that Pym patronized a group of educational reformers like Hartlib and Comenius in 1640–2. But Bacon himself was a royalist conservative, and the group of scientists who assembled in Wadham College, Oxford, in the 1650s seem to have been religious latitudinarians and political moderates rather than Puritans and radicals.[141] If there is any direct connection between scientific progress and political radicalism in the early seventeenth century it is most likely to have taken the form of patterns of reinforcement, a loose association of ideas for educational reform with ideas for political reform. But even this is by no means certain, and the only plausible hypothesis that can be advanced at present is that Baconian insistence on putting accepted dogmas about nature to empirical test, and the theoretical implications of some of the scientific discoveries, between them contributed to a mood of doubt and questioning.

This corrosion of authority was not confined only to secular affairs, but also spread to religion. The mere existence within a society of a number of actively competing religious sects and churches inevitably raised the question: What is the right road to salvation? To this the answer might be: Any; or even perhaps none. If toleration is bred of indifference, indifference is bred of religious pluralism. As the religious fanatics on all sides shouted louder and louder as they peddled their wares, so more and more sober men began to adopt a latitudinarian attitude of watchful scepticism, and to transfer their allegiance from the competing churches and sects to the secular State. Among the faithful, on the other hand, confidence in doctrine declined, to be compensated for by a rise in loyalty to the group, the sect or the congregation of the Independent Church.[142]

The result of this two-pronged attack on established beliefs was a real crisis of confidence in the early seventeenth century. As Drayton wrote in 1625 'Certainly there's scarce one found that now knows what to approve or what to disallow.'[143] The effect on the historical process of this mood of generalized anxiety and confusion cannot be neatly documented; but it is reasonable to suppose that it played its part in undermining confidence in the established institutions of Church and State.

The impact of these religious, intellectual and ideological forces was enormously increased by the dislocation and disturbance experienced by almost all sections of society. The social structure was under great stress, as a result of the doubling of the population, the sixfold increase in prices, the opening up of the land-market by the sale of monastic property, the growth of trade and industry, and the reorganization of agricultural production and distribution. This all led to what was generally regarded as a dangerously excessive degree of mobility among nearly all groups. In the early seventeenth century, families and individuals were moving at an unprecedented pace both geographically from village to village and from country-side to town, and vertically upward and downward in the social scale. Some roughly comparable statistical evidence is now available to demonstrate the speed with which landed families were disappearing and emerging in several counties during this period. Only Kent shows any degree of stability since of the gentry families extant in 1640 75 per cent were established there before 1485. But this was the exception. Less than 43 per cent of the families of Norfolk and Yorkshire in 1640 were of pre-Tudor origin, and less than 33 per cent of those of Suffolk, Northants, Essex, and Herts.[144] Other statistical information about the transfer of manors suggests that the period 1540–1640 was unique in English history between 1080 and 1880 for the speed with which these properties changed hands.[145] There were more gentry both rising and falling between 1540 and 1640 than at almost any other time in English history.

This remarkable social mobility in the upper ranks of society was paralleled by even more startling geographical mobility among the lower orders. In rural villages at this time the annual migration rate seems to have been as high as 5 per cent a year. Out of 166 individuals born in one Warwickshire parish in the early seventeenth century, 24 per cent died in infancy, and a further 44 per cent left the village without producing any children. Much of this migration was of adolescents acting as servants in homes of others, and often moving from year to year, but a good deal of it was of adults and whole families. In one Sussex example of the not wholly impoverished rural classes, a majority of adult males (6 out of 10) lived in more than one parish during their lives, and 1 in 6 lived in 3 or more. Although almost half did not move further than 5 miles, 1 in 10 travelled over 30 miles. This long-distance mobility finds confirmation in the apprenticeship records of the towns, which at this time were drawing recruits from an unusually wide area. For example, in the late sixteenth and early seventeenth centuries, London was drawing considerable numbers of immigrants from the North, whereas by the eighteenth century recruitment was largely confined to the home counties.[146] The causes of this remarkable pattern of migration must lie partly in the massive increase of population in the villages, the surplus of which were forced to move from economic necessity, partly in the social practice of putting children out to work in other people's homes from the age of about fourteen, and partly in the social upheaval in agriculture and the fluid conditions of property ownership, especially copyhold tenure.

The effects of this unprecedentedly widespread geographical mobility were compounded by the demographic uncertainties of the age. Town after town and village after village were repeatedly struck by plague or fever which tore at the very roots of the society. Barely half the country dwellers and hardly any inhabitants of towns could hope to live out their lives in a community which did not experience at least one of these psychologically devastating events, during which anything between a third and a half of the population would die in a matter of months.[147] To the shock of sudden loss of family, friends and neighbours was added the subsequent economic dislocation, with a large proportion of the community thrown out of work and dependent on charity for survival.

Given the traditional and conservative value system of the age, this great increase in mobility of all kinds in the hundred years from 1540 to 1640 created discontent rather than satisfaction, due primarily to the wide discrepancies which developed between the three sectors of wealth, status and power. Social discontent was felt by both the upwardly and the downwardly mobile. One economically rising group, the merchants, felt themselves denied social prestige in a society where the ownership of land was the criterion of status, and they resented the affront. Other economically advancing groups, the successful lawyers and the greater squires, felt themselves excluded from power by the Court, and also resented the affront. Of the declining groups, the wage-earners, squeezed between rising prices and lagging wages, were in a state of abject misery which found intermittent relief in rioting and mob-violence. The clergy lamented their loss of income and status relative to those of the laity, and under Laud they allied themselves with the Crown in a vain attempt to recover both. The plight of the third downwardly mobile group was even more pitiable. Over-educated and under-endowed, the younger sons of the gentry were condemned by the laws of primogeniture to slide down the social scale, unless they could save themselves by their exertions. But for those who opted for a career in one of the professions rather than in trade, the chances of success turned against them in the early seventeenth century, as the limited openings became clogged with an excess of aspirants. To many of these unfortunates, the Civil War must have come as welcome relief to a hopeless situation: they rushed to enroll as officers in both armies. In a changing and increasingly affluent society even stability was no guarantee of satisfaction. Personally insecure but static as a group, the small parish gentry resented their stagnation and were consumed with envy at the conspicuous success of merchants, courtiers and squires. Those nearest London felt the resentment most keenly, since they were most aware of the discrepancy in opportunities. Though the gentry of the home counties were better off economically than those of the north and west, they were more bitter since they knew what they were missing. Hence the loyalty to Church and King of the poor backwoodsmen of the west and north in the Civil War, and the rallying to the Independent cause of a section of the small gentry of the home counties.

At all levels, therefore, there was a sense of insecurity. In the upper ranks of society high social mobility generated jealousy, envy and despair among the failures, and status anxiety among the successful. In the lower ranks extraordinary geographic mobility and periodic catastrophes due to epidemic disease, combined to shatter the traditional ties to family, kin, and neighbours, and to wrench men away from their familiar associations and surroundings.

At the very same time the ideological props of their universe were falling away. Competing religious ideologies shattered the unquestioning and habit-forming faith of the past; the failure of the Anglican Church to put its house in order left it open to every enterprising undergraduate to draw up an alternative scheme for ecclesiastical organization; constitutional conflicts between Commons and Crown disturbed conventional notions of the role of the State and posed the insoluble question of sovereignty; the collapse of the quasi-feudal ties of hereditary dependence left men free to seek clientage where they could find it; the decline of the craft guilds freed labour from both rules and companionship; the bonds of kinship were loosened under pressure from new religious and political associations, and from new ideals of love and freedom within the nuclear family. The upsetting of the heirarchy of status as a result of rapid social mobility was thus just one of many factors which generated unease, anxiety, anomie. Social mobility, personal insecurity, geographical migration, and ideological chaos were all part of the life experiences of early seventeenth-century Englishmen. They were all deeply unsettling.

Another disturbing factor was the growing realization that the numbers of the leisured class equipped with higher education were increasing faster than the suitable job opportunities. The extraordinary expansion of enrolments in Oxford and Cambridge meant the creation of a small army of unemployed or under-employed gentry whose training had equipped them for positions of responsibility, but for whom the avenues of opportunity were clogged. Neither the central bureaucracy, nor the army, nor colonial expansion in Ireland, nor even the law could absorb them all. The result was frustration and resentment amoug large numbers of nobles, squires and gentry. Second, the Universities were turning out degree-holding clergy in numbers well in excess of the capacity of the Church to absorb them. They flooded into low-paid curacies with little prospects of promotion, so that by 1635 in the Oxford diocese 98 per cent of all curates held degrees. Fifty years before in the diocese of Worcester not a single curate held a degree.[148] Many other graduates filled lectureships in the towns, and a few got themselves taken on as private chaplains in noble households. All were resentful of a society which had over-trained them and could not employ them, and many naturally drifted into religious and political radicalism. The lecturers in the towns were an especially subversive body, operating outside the normal structure of clerical organization and hierarchy and with an enormous popular following. They were the seventeenth-century equivalent of the medieval friars, but over-educated friars with families to support, embittered by their failure to break into the fat pastures of high clerical preferment, for which their education and talents fitted them.

One result of this educational over-expansion, coupled with the development and spread of a series of ideologies antagonistic to the *status quo*, was the appearance of that sinister precursor of a time of political troubles, the alienation of the intellectuals.[149] The Puritan ministers and lecturers in the cities and the villages, some dons behind the greying walls of their colleges, many common lawyers at the Inns of Court, all increasingly felt themselves cut off in spirit and in reality from the central institutions of government. In so highly literate a society as that of early seventeenth-century England, this alienation of many members of the most articulate segments boded no good for the regime. Moreover this was merely one aspect of the wider phenomenon of a deepening split between two cultures, one represented by the bulk of the political nation, and the other by a minority at Court and among the higher clergy and judges. It was a split which was symbolized by the emergence of clearly antithetical myths and ideologies: Obedience versus Conscience; the Divine Right of Kings versus the Balanced Constitution; the Beauty of Holiness versus Puritan austerity; Court versus Country.

Conclusion

To sum up this survey of preconditions, one can see that by the 1620s England was moving into a condition of disequilibrium, or multiple dysfunction. New social forces were emerging, new political relationships were forming, and new intellectual currents were flowing, but neither the secular government nor the Church was demonstrating an ability to adapt to new circumstances. Thanks to the growth of the national product, the changing distribution of wealth, the spread of higher education, the decline of aristocratic political dominance on local affairs, the formulation of new religious and secular ideals, and the consolidation of new administrative organizations, in the century after 1540, there appeared a growing body of men of substance, rich property owners, professionals and merchants. These men – the leading figures among the county squirarchy, the successful London lawyers, the more eminent Puritan divines, and the urban patriciates that dominated the cities

– were steadily enlarging their numbers, their social and economic weight, and their political independence. Behind them loomed far larger numbers of yeomen and artisans, the respectable, industrious, literate, bible-reading, God-fearing lower middle class, many of whose aspirations these leaders shared, represented and articulated.

These men were not only seeking a larger voice in political affairs and the right to consent to taxation. They were also asking for change: for a reform of court morals, financial and personal, an overtly Protestant foreign policy, a moderate purification of Church ritual and a diminution of episcopal authority. The only response they got was increasingly strident and irrelevant lectures on the Divine Right of Kings; the promotion to power of a group of clergy whose aim was to increase the importance of Church ritual and to increase the authority of the episcopacy; the obstinate pursuit of the chimera of the Spanish Marriage as the central objective of foreign policy; and ever more blatant corruption, extravagance and incompetence at Court under the leadership of George Villiers, Duke of Buckingham, the youthful darling of the doting and drink-sodden old King, and the bosom friend of his austere young heir.

This analysis of the various features in a deteriorating situation conceals one very important point, which is that the very success of the Elizabethan policy of cautious compromise and artful procrastination was an important source of trouble to the Stuarts. In the first place, the successful avoidance of internal violence bred over-confidence among the propertied classes in their ability to steer a steady course between the Scylla of docile obedience to the exorbitant demands of the Crown, and the Charybdis of the unleashing of civil war. In the Church, the Elizabethan policy of studied indifference to spiritual matters had allowed the Puritan preachers and the Catholic priests to capture the hearts and minds of some of the best and most educated elements of the population. In finance, the Elizabethan policy of turning a blind eye to widespread tax-evasion by the landed classes, and gross under-assessment of customs by the merchant community, led directly to a constitutional crisis as soon as the Stuarts tried to remedy an intolerable situation. In Parliament, Elizabeth had thoughtlessly allowed the numbers in the House of Commons to increase alarmingly. She fought for her prerogative inch by inch and step by step, but she adopted the ill-advised tactics of evasive ambiguity on fundamental issues which should and could have been clarified, together with intransigence on specific issues such as the succession, moderate Church reform and monopolies, which should and could have been compromised or conceded. The combination merely encouraged the Parliamentary gentry to formulate even more aggressive demands for constitutional change. 'Love-tricks' were all very well in the short run, but they were no substitute for a consistent policy, and it was these opportunist and short-sighted tactics which justify the harsh conclusion that she was 'the splendid though involuntary betrayer of the cause of monarchy'.[150] By 1653 a Fifth Monarchist could report that, with the hindsight of half a century, 'some compare Queen Elizabeth to a sluttish house-wife, who swept the house but left the dust behind the door.'[151] Many of the troubles of the Stuarts were directly caused by the tactical successes of Elizabeth, and her studied avoidance of dealing with the underlying problems. She won many battles, but died before losing the war.

The essential thrust of this historical analysis has been to stress the interconnection of forces and events, to demonstrate the way every-thing affects, and is affected by, everything else. But if one were forced to identify the most salient elements in the manifold pre-conditions which have been described, four would have to singled out as of prime importance. The first was the failure of the Crown to acquire two key instruments of power, a standing army and a paid, reliable local bureaucracy. Second comes the decline of the aristo-cracy, and the corresponding rise of the gentry: a rise partly in terms of relative wealth, status, education, adminstrative experience, and group identity in county government, and partly in terms of political self-confidence on the floor of the House of Commons as the repre-sentatives of a 'Country' ideology. Third, there was the spread throughout large sectors of the propertied and lower middle classes of a diffuse Puritanism, whose most important political consequence was to create a burning sense of the need for change in the Church and eventually in the State. Last but not least was the growing crisis of confidence in the integrity and moral worth of the holders of high administrative office, whether courtiers or nobles or bishops or judges or even kings.

The most important secondary factors were the spread of educa-tion at every level; the independent power of the common lawyers and their 'Magna Carta' ideology; the progressive transformation of the economy, with the commercialization of agriculture and rural social relationships, the growth of overseas trade and industry, and the doubling of the population; the false sense of security caused by the initial success of Elizabethan compromise; and the increased size and cost, coupled with the deterioration in efficiency and integrity, of the central organs of government and the Court. It must be stressed that none of the factors here listed made the collapse of government inevitable, much less the outbreak of civil war or the rise of a genuinely revolutionary political party. These preconditions made some redistribution of political power almost inevitable, and reform of the Church very probable, but whether these changes would come about by peaceful evolution, political upheaval, or force of arms was altogether uncertain, dependent on the wisdom, or lack of it, of the government, and the moderation, or lack of it, of the opposition.

3. The precipitants, 1629–39

Every historian is obliged to follow his own judgment in the role he ascribes in historical causation to accident and to individual personality. Few would deny that the individual political leader is severely circumscribed in his freedom of action by the objective conditions in which he finds himself. Moreover the leader is moulded in his values and opinions by the socialization process he has undergone, which in turn is prescribed by social and cultural determinants. And finally he has a following and a set of associates whose aspirations and interests he must satisfy. When all is said and done, however, it is difficult to avoid the conclusion that, although the broad sweeps of history move in inexorable patterns, yet vitally important short-term decisions may none the less depend on the decision of an individual. This is particularly true in the case of a decision for war or peace, a decision which often in the past, and unquestionably today, has the most serious historical consequences.

The analysis of the causes of the English Revolution has hitherto dealt in forces and trends, social, economic, political and religious, and in long-term governmental policies. As we move from *structure* to *conjuncture*, however, we must increasingly lay stress on the options open to individuals, and on the consequences of the choices they made. When dealing with the last two years before the outbreak of war, the principal stress will be on the leading actors and their behaviour in moments of crisis. To pass judgment upon the results of these decisions necessarily involves the postulating, if only secretly and even unconsciously, of a counter-factual proposition:

what would have happened if X had decided differently? No logical scientific defence can be offered for such a procedure, but merely the weak argument that it seems to make sense to the working historian.

During the decade before the crash in 1640, a series of developments took place which may be regarded as precipitants of crisis, for they brought the collapse of governmental institutions from the realm of possibility to that of probability. The main emphasis must be placed upon the folly and intransigence of the government, its blind refusal to respond constructively to criticism, and its obstinate departure upon a collision course. Most contemporaries would have agreed that the opposition leaders had gone too far in 1629 in refusing the Crown even its traditional right to levy customs and in holding down the Speaker while they forced through some extravagantly worded resolutions of defiance. The Duke of Buckingham, whom many had come to view as the source of all evil in the nation, was now dead, and many hoped for a reconciliation and a healing of the wounds. But the ruthless and uncompromising nature of the royal policies after 1629 steadily drove more and more of the silent majority into the arms of the opposition.

In the first place the Crown associated itself whole-heartedly with a vigorous religious reaction guided and driven furiously forward by Archbishop Laud.[152] The latter saw Church and State as two beleaguered garrisons which needed to unite against their enemies, and by cementing the alliance he ensured that the fall of the one would inevitably drag the other down with it. As early as 1625 he warned the critics of the Established Church that 'They, whoever they be, that would overthrow *Sedes Ecclesiae*, the seats of ecclesiastical government, will not spare (if ever they get power) to have a pluck at the throne of David.' This might be thought a shrewd insight into the future, were it not that Laud's own actions in the next fifteen years did much to ensure that it was a self-fulfilling prophecy. His view of the relationship between Church and State is well illustrated by the instructions issued by his vicar-general, Sir Nathaniel Brent, to the church of Boston, Lincs., during an archiepiscopal visitation. He ordered the walls of the church to be 'adorned with devout and holy sentences of Scripture . . . divers of which sentences shall tend to the exhortation of the people to obedience to the King's most excellent majesty'.[153]

An important element in Laud's plans was the recovery of the political power and the prestige of the bishops after decades of neglect and contempt. Bishops re-appeared in strength in the Privy Council, and one, Juxon, actually became Lord Treasurer, the first since the Reformation; in cathedral towns bishops began a vigorous reassertion of their rights and financial privileges against the secular authorities; bishops played a more active role on the bench of justices; opponents and slanderers of bishops were silenced by savage mutilation and close imprisonment. Serious efforts were made to recover some of the economic resources of the Church which had been lost over the previous century. An attack was launched on urban tithes in London, since if the Church could collect anything approaching 10 per cent of the annual rental value of urban properties, its fortunes would be well on the way to recoveiy. Measures were taken to prevent more impropriations of livings from falling into the hands of Puritan patrons, and plans were developed for a broad assault on lay control of clerical tithes and clerical patronage. In the forms of worship, stress was laid on the revival of hieratic ritual and visual ornament, in ways which had not been seen for over sixty years. Communion tables were put back in the east end of churches, and protected by altar rails; the erection of organs and stained-glass windows was encouraged; the clergy were ordered to use the surplice and the laity to kneel at the altar rails to receive the sacrament.

These measures were accompanied and supported by a counter-revolution in theology, taking the form of a hostility to the Calvinist predestinarian determinism which had been common to all parties in the Elizabethan Church. The greater stress on free grace that these 'Arminian' views entailed soon took on the tinge of sacramentalism, of a stress on the role of the clergyman as the intercessor and mediator between God and man. Gone was the priesthood of all believers, once the clergyman in his surplice had retreated behind the altar rails to administer the sacraments necessary to salvation.

The improved intellectual, moral, social and perhaps economic conditions of the lower clergy served in other ways to increase tensions with the laity. The Caroline parish clergy were now certainly a long way removed from the peasantry with whom they had been assimilated before the Reformation. Their educational background was now quite different from that of their parishioners, for their outlook on the world had been moulded by the experience of the university and the dignity of a degree, a dignity which carried with it implications of gentle status. It may well be that clerical incomes were rising in the early seventeenth century as a result of increased legal pressure through the courts for the full payment of tithes. This litigation increased the incomes but decreased the popularity of the clergy. Third, the improvement in standards created friction with the gentry as well as with the poor parishioners. In the days of Elizabeth the Puritan gentry had been demanding above all else an educated clergy, but the moment they got one they began talking about the virtues of simple sermons in plain language without all the scholarly paraphernalia picked up at Oxbridge. The Caroline lower clergy may still have been drawn from the lower middle classes – or increasingly from the clergy itself as a hereditary profession – but their life-style and their pretensions were rising and they were moving in the direction of closer social identification with the landed classes. The inevitable if unforeseen result of giving an elaborate scholastic education to a socially insecure but ambitious body of clergy was that they developed first Laudian then Presbyterian claims to clerical authority. In the 1630s and 1640s the clergy regarded themselves as competitors with the gentry for leadership, and first clerical Arminianism and then clerical Presbyterianism were both of them serious threats to the doggedly Erastian laity. Both were defeated, but it was not until after the Restoration that the clergy took their place as docile associates of the gentry at college, at the table, and in the hunting field, men who could be relied upon to know their place and act accordingly. Their social status had risen and their political aspirations declined, so that they were now acceptable partners of the gentry in the tasks of social control.

Those who expressed disagreement with Laudian measures or doctrines were harried and persecuted with a ruthless persistence which was worse than in the days of Whitgift – so ruthless indeed that thousands fled across 3,000 miles of ocean to the wilderness of Massachusetts. Ruthless though it was, however, it was not ruthless enough. Laud may have driven thousands to America, he may have silenced his more obstreperous enemies, but thousands more – like Oliver Cromwell – remained at home to nurse their grievances and plan revenge. Moreover, most of the Puritan lecturers contrived to survive the persecution. These lecturers in the towns, and especially London, were the principal propaganda agents for the opposition, and every effort was made to suppress them. As a Laudian official remarked in 1636 'if his Majesty shall in his princely care abolish that ratsbane of lecturing out of his churches, we shall have such a uniform and orthodox Church as the Christian World cannot show the like.' But the congregations, who were the patrons and paymasters of the London lecturers, offered them protection, and at the height of the Laudian persecution some forty-six Puritan lecturers were still delivering some sixty sermons a week within the square mile of the City.[154] Equally striking was the abject failure of Laud's strenuous parallel attempts to enforce the laws which prohibited the printing and publication of any book without a licence. During the 1630s, when the pressures for enforcement were at their most intense, only one third of the books published had passed through the licensing process.[155] Faced with opponents who, both as authors and as ministers, found protection under the wing of influential lay patrons, and lacking the necessary bureaucratic machinery in either Church or State, Laud was unable to enforce his will. The best he could achieve was brutal punishment of a handful of offenders, which merely served to exasperate the others.

The gap between the realities of the situation and the description of it offered to the King in the annual reports drawn up by Laud is so wide as to suggest the development of an alarming failure of communication between government and people.[156] The reports note minor difficulties and individual dissenters here and there, some trouble from the inhabitants of some of the Kentish towns, and the perennial problem of the poverty of many of the parish clergy. But in general they describe a situation fully under control, and a population generally devout, orthodox, obedient and loyal. Unless we are to conclude that the Archbishop was deliberately deceiving his King, he must have been wholly out of touch with what was really happening. His impotence was compounded by his ignorance.

Even more harmful to Laudian ambitions than the weakness of the powers of repression was the growing suspicion that the policy was intended to end in the full restoration of Roman Catholicism. This suspicion was assiduously fanned by the Puritan opposition, and the cynical John Selden confessed that 'We charge the prelatical clergy of popery to make them odious, though we know they are guilty of no such thing.' Selden may have known this, but the public was more gullible. From the Gunpowder Plot to the Popish Plot, the English in the seventeenth century were paranoid in their fear and hatred of popery. This made it easy for Puritans and others to destroy their political enemies with smear campaigns based on vague charges of guilt by association. The accusation that Laud was leading England towards popery was supported by a series of apparently sinister developments, which provided a good deal of plausibly circumstantial evidence. There was the clear and growing influence exerted over Charles by his Catholic Queen; the employment of

Catholic laymen like Windebank in high ministerial offices; the amiable relations maintained with the Papacy, which was allowed to establish an agent in London; the pursuit of a foreign policy which seemed blatantly pro-Spanish and anti-Protestant; and the construction of a costly and ostentatiously Counter-Reformation baroque Catholic chapel in St James's Palace. Popular perceptions are often more important than reality, and, given the hysterical fears of the time, the suspicion that the administration was indelibly tarnished with popery had catastrophic effects on public confidence in the regime. A royal supporter remarked in 1640 that 'the people being persuaded or of opinion that their leaders and service were Popish has done his Majesty more disservice than any one thing', a judgment escalated by a radical M.P. to the charge that: 'the root of all our grievances I think to be an intended union between us and Rome.'[157] This suspicion was the main cause of the refusal of the troops to fight the Scots, which led directly to the downfall of the regime, and of the lack of trust which made a subsequent settlement impossible.

Parallel to this reaction in religion was a reaction in politics, in the degree of participation allowed to the traditional freeholder electorate and the traditional gentry representatives. As early as 1626 Charles had bluntly announced that 'Parliaments are altogether in my power for the calling, sitting, and dissolution. Therefore, as I find the fruits of them good or evil they are to continue or not to be.'[158] Three years later he dissolved Parliament and proclaimed his intention of ruling without it. He then proceeded to raise taxes without consent by juggling with the letter of the law and by perverting residual prerogative powers of the Crown for emergency action in moments of national danger. Medieval precedents were dredged up to allow the Crown to fine very large numbers of the gentry for their failure to take up knighthood, and to fine selected numbers of noblemen for ancient encroachments on the royal forests – a move which involved a serious challenge to the right of title to property. The authority to levy money for ships in a national emergency from the port towns was converted into a nation-wide annual tax in times of peace, which affected most of the population right down to the small freeholder and shopkeeper. Receipts from wardship, that arbitrary inheritance tax which was an obsolete relic of feudalism, were trebled in a decade.[159] But it was still not enough. One of the difficulties was that the desire to maximize revenues ran counter to the desire to strengthen royal authority, check corruption and ensure social stability. The latter motive worked against any further exploitation of Buckingham's policies of selling offices and titles to the highest bidder, and of manipulating industrial and commercial monopolies to benefit a selected minority of courtiers.[160] On some issues like the punishment of enclosers, the desire to raise revenue by fining the guilty was directly opposed to the desire to prevent the practice itself as socially undesirable.

Besides this conflict between financial interest and social responsibility, there was the further problem created by the absence of a satisfactory system of long-term government credit. Without a bank from which to borrow, the Crown was forced to rely on a line of credit extended to it by the farmers of the Customs in return for favourable contracts, and was also forced as a matter of routine to delay indefinitely the settlement of current bills for the purchase of supplies.[161] But these practices drove up the administrative overheads, since the customs farmers naturally took their profits, and everyone who did business with the government padded their bills in order to make allowance for the long delays in payment. The result was that the Crown was obliged to raise money by devices which involved a high economic cost in terms of real interest rates, and a high political cost in terms of the alienation of potential supporters. But the sums raised were still not sufficient to enable it to expand its military forces and administrative staff to the levels required if it was to establish its authoritarian power on a secure basis.

The fiscal policies of the 1630s caused formidable opposition, not because royal taxation was particularly oppressive to any class of society – indeed it was quite certainly lighter than anywhere else in Europe – but because the money was levied in an unconstitutional and arbitrary manner, and was used for purposes which many taxpayers regarded as immoral. Gentry claims to participation in political decision-making, and particularly to consent to taxation, were no longer recognized by Charles, as was made brutally clear in his Proclamation of 27 March 1629, in which he stated his intention to rule for a long time to come without consultation of Parliament. As the years of authoritarian rule dragged on, the full significance of his words became even more apparent:[162]

we shall account it presumption for any to prescribe any time unto us for parliaments, the calling, continuing and dissolving of which is always in our own power; and we shall be more inclinable to meet in parliament again when our people shall see more clearly into our intentions and actions, when such as

have bred this interruption shall have received their condign
punishment, and those who are misled by them and by such
ill reports as are raised upon this occasion shall come to a
better understanding of themselves and us.

This attack on the national authority of the greater gentry as
M.P.s, through the suspension of Parliament and the raising of taxes
by non-Parliamentary means, was paralleled by an attack on their
local authority as J.P.s through increasingly tight supervision from
London. The pressure began with the imposition of the forced loan
of 1626–7, and became much worse with the issuing of the Book of
Orders of 1630, which closely regulated their proceedings, and with
the subsequent swelling stream of letters from the Privy Council,
instructing, rebuking, exhorting, and demanding detailed reports on
all their activities. Their pride was wounded by the forcible addition
of clergymen to the bench, and the last straw came when they were
told to assist in the hateful task of assessing and collecting ship
money from a recalcitrant population whose constitutional objections they fully shared. From 1625 onwards the J.P.s found themselves on the one hand burdened down with the ever-increasing
weight of tedious and time-consuming administrative chores, and
on the other more and more closely circumscribed in their freedom
of action, and more and more obliged to execute policies they personally detested. In the late 1630s things had become so bad that
growing numbers of leading gentry were refusing to take their
natural place on the bench, a process which in the long run might
have paralysed the working of government at the local level.[163]

The political authority of the aristocracy was also deteriorating,
since the House of Lords was affected, along with the House of
Commons, by the decision of the King to rule without Parliament.
What one sees in the 1620s and 1630s is the emergence of a kind of
aristocratic constitutionalism which sought to revive the medieval
tradition of noble opposition to central bureaucratic administration.
One aspect of this movement was the revival by the opposition
lawyers of the practice of impeachment, by which leading ministers
were brought to trial before the House of Lords on charges presented
by the House of Commons. There are some signs that in the 1620s
Sir Edward Coke was trying to manipulate the House of Lords into
adopting a mediating role in the growing constitutional crisis, after
he had failed in his attempt to elevate the judges into such a position.
The constitutional thinking of Puritan aristocrats like Essex was

not so very different, but their ambitions were doomed to failure.[164] The Crown was anxious enough to enhance the social prestige of the nobles in order to put the gentry in their place, but was unwilling to set them up as watchdogs over the new bureaucratic state. As for the gentry, it became very clear in 1640, and indeed before, that although they needed aristocratic leadership, they were now quite unwilling to subordinate either themselves or their House.

Relative deprivation theory is usually applied to economic goods, but in fact it works equally well, or even better, when applied to political goods, namely a share in decision-making. For nearly a century up to 1629 the political influence of the greater gentry had been increasing, while the great Puritan peers had had a considerable stake at Court in the first thirty years of Elizabeth's reign, and had still been influential for most of the reign of James. In the 1630s both groups were deprived of powers which they had come to regard as a right. The 'J-curve' theory of revolution, which emphasizes the importance of the discrepancy between constantly rising expectations and first rising and then falling capacities, is directly applicable to the changing distribution of political power in national and local government.

In addition to a religious and a political reaction, Charles and his advisers also set out to enforce a social reaction, to put the lid on the social mobility he found so distasteful. In 1629 he abruptly ended the practice of sale of titles which had been flourishing since 1616, he drove the gentry and nobility out of London back to their rural retreats where he thought they belonged, and he did all he could to bolster up noble privileges and to reinforce the hierarchy of ranks.[165] He increased the proportion of second generation noblemen in the Privy Council, he severely punished anyone who insulted aristocrats, he restricted access to the Privy Chamber according to rank, and some of his advisers considered the idea of attaching political and financial privilege to titles on the continental model. The logical culmination of this attitude was the summoning of a medieval Great Council in 1640 to advise the king on how to deal with the crisis caused by the defeat in the Scottish Wars. The noblemen themselves were busy writing or commissioning family histories, elaborating their coats of arms, and pushing their genealogies farther and farther back into a remote and improbable antiquity, while at the same time many of them were instructing their agents to exploit to the full the financial profits to be derived from a revival of long-forgotten feudal dues. Taken together, Crown policies and noble behaviour strongly suggest the beginnings of an aristocratic social reaction which might in time have developed into something comparable to the more self-conscious and comprehensive movement in France in the decades before the French Revolution. This latter is thought to have played an important part in heightening the social tensions which finally led to the explosion in 1789, and it seems reasonable to suppose that the admittedly less well-developed reaction in England aroused similar resentments among the gentry. It played its part in stimulating among the members of the Lower House that hostility to and suspicion of the House of Lords which is so evident a feature of even the early sessions of the Long Parliament.

Lastly Charles got himself involved in economic reaction. Guild organization was imposed from above on numerous crafts and trades, the purpose of which was to establish strict royal control over the industrial and artisan class of small masters – a clear case of Colbertism before Colbert;[166] an ever-growing host of offensive and useless monopolies were strictly enforced, and attempts were made to tighten regulations governing the quality of cloth;[167] fines were imposed on the squirarchy for violations of the anti-enclosure laws.[168] Important and growing commercial interests outside the urban élite were frustrated by the refusal of the government to give any encouragement to an anti-Spanish commercial policy of interloping and privateering in the Americas. Every aspect of economic life suffered from the feverish interference of a bureaucracy whose sole objective seemed to be the extraction of money by the imposition of a multitude of petty and irritating regulations, many of which were of dubious legality.

In short, the objective of 'Thorough' was a deferential, strictly hierarchical, socially stable, paternalist absolutism based on a close union of Church and Crown. It involved a rejection of any concessions to the opposition; no co-option of potential opposition leaders; actions and statements in domestic and foreign policy which gave the maximum offence to the sensibilities and interests of important individuals and groups; and a persecution which created martyrs in dozens and exiles in thousands, but left the heart of the opposition untouched.

While these policies were being implemented, the governing élites began to split apart, so that the reaction had to be carried out by a regime already half at war with itself. In the administration, the new advocates of efficiency, austerity and discipline – self-styled

'Thorough' – fought the older, easy-going, routinely venal bureau-
crats, whom they dubbed 'Lady Mora'. In the Privy Council,
Protestants fought Catholics and crypto-Catholics. Laud and his
supporters fought Weston and the Queen. The loyalty of a host of
minor officials was undermined by the activities of the Commission
on Fees, which threatened their livelihood.[169] The aristocracy split
apart as more and more were ejected from or refused to come to
Court, and some drifted over to join, and indeed to lead, the opposition. The episcopal bench was split, as Laud and his Arminian allies
fought Bishop Williams and his friends, for by no means all the
bishops welcomed the extension of archiepiscopal influence in the
administration of their dioceses. Many of the lay courtiers and
officials were jealous of the increasing interference by the bishops in
secular administration and policy.

Some of the most self-interested supporters of the Crown were the
merchant oligarchies which controlled the political and economic life
of the towns.[170] The loyalty of these oligarchies, and especially that of
London, was to be of decisive political importance in the crisis years
ahead, but their devotion was severely strained by royal policies
towards them in the late 1620s and the 1630s, which were oppor-
tunistic, grasping, selfish and rude. In the first place, the royal
advisers tried the patience and goodwill of the urban élites to the
limits in order to squeeze the maximum short-term fiscal advantages
out of them. Thus the City of London was bullied ruthlessly over the
Londonderry Plantation it had undertaken, over the Crown lands
it had agreed to sell on contract, and over its claims to title to old
chantry property. The Levant Company in 1628–9 saw some thirty of
its leading members thrown into jail for refusing to pay an arbitrary
increase in the imposition on imported currants. The rapid expansion
of monopolistic licensing merely served to multiply the points of
friction between different monopolists, and to exasperate all parties.
The Greenland Company and the Eastland Company resented the
Soap-boilers monopoly, the East India Company resented the gunpowder monopoly and the licensing of interlopers like the Courteen
Company; the Merchant Adventurers Company resented the Duke
of Lennox's license to export white cloths. The imposition of guild
organization on industrial crafts merely compounded the difficulties
by adding to the frictions between organized and competing interest
groups. Finally, the growing royal habit of interfering in the internal
affairs of the various companies inevitably bred resentment and
resistance. These irritants were not sufficient to turn the élite of the

City against the government, since their self-interest outweighed their discontents. After all, it was from the Crown that they obtained the town charters which gave them their political power, and the company charters which gave them their economic power. But the experience of the past decade was sufficient to blunt their enthusiasm to rush to Charles's rescue when he had his back to the wall in 1640. When he turned to them for a massive loan in order to carry on without Parliament, they were psychologically sufficiently alienated to be prepared to refuse. Strafford's characteristically brutal suggestion that some of the more recalcitrant aldermen should be hanged *pour encourager les autres* did nothing to improve the Crown's relations with the City. The refusal to advance a loan was undoubtedly mainly caused by serious doubts about the value of the security for the loan which could be offered by a government which had already pledged its revenues several years in advance, but the mistreatment they had suffered over the previous fifteen years undoubtedly made it easier for the Mayor and Aldermen to reject the royal request. Their refusal caused the downfall of the regime, and compelled the summoning of Parliament.[171] The fact that in the end the City magnates came to realize that their fate and that of the monarchy were inextricably bound up together does nothing to alter the fact that, partly because of royal policies, at the critical moment they failed to come to the aid of the Crown.

While the interests and groups supporting the Crown were beginning to weaken in their loyalties and even to split apart, royal tactics and strategy were at last achieving something which none of the opposition leaders of the 1620s, not Coke, not Eliot, had been able to achieve: they were welding together the nationally disparate forces of opposition.

The most striking result of the Crown's religious policies was paradoxically to stimulate an enormous growth in Puritan sentiment. Laud may justly be regarded as the most important single contributor to the cause of Puritanism in the early seventeenth century, a classic example of the way in which so often in history concrete results do not merely fall short of the objectives of political actors, but are actually their diametrical opposites. Beginning in the 1590s, the professional theologians had started a controversy over issues of little concern to any but themselves. While the lawyers in the Inns of Court were squabbling amongst themselves over the powers of the common law and the prerogative courts, the dons at Oxford and Cambridge were tearing each other apart over obscure interpretations of the doctrine of Grace.[172] But just as the legal battle eventually became politicized and shifted to Parliament in the 1620s, so did the quarrel between Calvinists and Arminians. The Crown hesitated between the two for a long time, but the latter were the most extreme partisans of the Divine Right of Kings, and of the authority of the Church as an ally of the Crown. And so in the mid-1620s Buckingham and Charles finally threw all their influence and patronage behind the Arminians, and the Calvinists appealed to the House of Commons for help in suppressing these novel and divisive doctrines. Arminian theology became associated with clerical self-assertion and the royal prerogative, and the laity were forced to take sides. Religious opinion in the country was polarized, since the moderate and fairly tolerant episcopacy that had been dominant in the Church in the first half of Elizabeth's reign and again under James was now extruded from power. The assumption by Laud and his allies that whoever was anti-Arminian was therefore Puritan became a self-fulfilling prophecy: within ten years they succeeded in creating a new, large, and radical Puritan party out of the hard core of the old one plus a mass of now alienated Anglicans still clinging to the Elizabethan traditions of Calvinism, Erastianism, and a minimum of ceremonial. The assertion of the power of bishops to enforce Laudian policies led directly to the emergence of an influential body of lay opinion which demanded the 'root and branch' abolition of episcopacy. As a direct result of Laudian activity, in 1641 Henry Parker observed that 'the world is full of nothing else but Puritans, for besides the Puritans in Church policy, there are now added Puritans in religion, Puritans in state, and Puritans in morality.'[173]

Just as the Anglican laity were forced into the camp of the Puritans, so the gentry, who harboured intensely ambivalent feelings towards the lawyers, were thrust into alliance with them by royal use of the prerogative courts and sycophantic judges to crush opposition and to impose taxation. The classic example of this is the abolition of Star Chamber, which, until it was perverted into a vehicle for punishing religious and political dissidents in the 1630s, had been a most popular and successful court, respected and frequented by crowds of litigants seeking the swift, cheap and fair justice that it offered. Some of the common lawyers had long disliked it for its equitable procedures and its careful attention to keeping fees low, but it was only when the gentry turned against it for political reasons that there was sufficient political support for its abolition.[174]

In order to break the electoral hold of the great courtiers, nobles and officials, the gentry found themselves obliged to encourage an expansion in the size of the electorate. Whatever their reservations about the perils of 'democracy' – which was a word with a strong pejorative connotation in the seventeenth century – they on all occasions voted to enlarge the body of electors and to extend the franchise to its legal limits. In doing so, they allied themselves with yeomen and artisans and encouraged them to claim their voting rights and to exercise them independently of the traditional political patrons. Opposition noblemen like Warwick built up a highly effective local electoral machine by the manipulation of this greatly enlarged electorate, but in general the significance of this expansion was to increase the independence of the voters from patronage, bribery, and manipulation. The emergence for a period of about one hundred years, from 1620 to 1720, of a very large and articulate electorate, preoccupied with issues and eventually organized around parties, is one of the most significant, and the least studied, constitutional developments of the seventeenth century.[175]

Leadership of the growing opposition was provided in the 1620s by Sir Edward Coke and Sir John Eliot, making the House of Commons their institutional base. In the 1630s when Parliament was suspended, other men and other institutions emerged. Pym, Hampden, Saye and Sele and Warwick took charge, and coherent organization at the top was achieved by the Providence Island Company directorate. The government in its folly gave the opposition its needed martyrs: first Sir John Eliot, imprisoned without trial for his actions in Parliament until he died, and whose corpse, in an act of petty posthumous revenge, Charles insisted on burying in the graveyard by the Tower of London rather than at home with his ancestors; then Burton, Bastwick and Prynne, who for their attacks on episcopacy were obliged to suffer the physical mutilations thought appropriate only for men of the lower classes. In all these cases the government was riding roughshod over the sense of what was a suitable penalty for a gentleman and what was not. The final stroke of royal folly was to allow all the different grievances of every malcontent in the kingdom to become focused onto a personal hatred of the persons and policies of two men, Strafford and Laud. The destruction of these two would, it was believed, purge the Commonwealth of the evils which were crushing it, and open the way to a better State and a better Church. This personalization of the issues enormously increased their popular appeal and facilitated the work of the Parliamentary leaders by giving their followers a clear destructive goal to work for. The hatred that eleven years before had been directed at the Duke of Buckingham had by 1640 been transferred to Strafford and Laud.

The final contribution to the erosion of consensus and the deterioration of political control was the fact that this conflict over fundamental constitutional, social and religious issues took place against a background of serious economic difficulties.[176] The main export trade in cloth had been dealt a shattering blow in the crisis of 1620–1 from which the European markets never really recovered. Moreover, the 1630s were generally a period of poor harvests, beginning with a catastrophic year, 1630, and continuing thereafter. There was only one good harvest in the decade, a situation for which there was to be only one parallel in the next hundred and twenty years.[177] The early seventeenth century therefore pursued the familiar 'J-curve' of a fairly long period of prosperity, which aroused expectations of continuing improvement, followed by a sharp downward turn. The reactionary royal policies of the 1630s were pursued at a time of frustrated economic expectations for many sectors of society.

On the other hand deteriorating financial conditions were definitely *not* a factor in arousing discontent among the landlord class, which was the main actor in the coming drama. Rents were soaring in the 1620s and 1630s, and taken as a whole the gentry, who with their aristocratic and London allies were to topple the government in 1640 and so set in motion the train of revolution, had never had it so good.[178] But the economic downswing helped to heighten tensions in the towns between the old-established monopolistic merchant oligarchies on the one hand, and on the other the pioneers in new markets, the interlopers in old markets, and the smaller traders, all of whom were excluded from the magic circle of power and privilege. Moreover the stagnation of the cloth trade must have helped to radicalize cloth workers, just as the high price of food must have stimulated the urban apprentices, especially in London, to political action in the streets. The role of the economic downswing was therefore a limited one, affecting only the urban classes from merchants to apprentices. The rural élite were largely unaffected, and the rural poor were to play little or no part in the coming political upheavals.

What was so menacing about royal policies, or appeared so to the fearful gentry of England, was the way they all fitted together to form a coherent whole. Most alarming of all was the way things were going in the two semi-colonial areas, where measures were being taken which many saw – not without reason – as a blue-print for later adoption in England itself.[179] In Ireland Strafford was deliberately and ruthlessly striking down all opposition, and was setting out to recover from the recent English gentry settlers the lost power and property of both Church and Crown. To do this he admitted that he was employing 'a little violence and extraordinary means'. In other words he was trampling on the law to expropriate the gentry, seizing from them the property and patronage they had acquired, by undoubtedly dubious means, over a generation ago in the great land-grab after the collapse of the Irish rebellion. He ignored the rights of common law to recover both land and impropriations of livings for the Crown and the Church.

When this authoritarian policy of Strafford in Ireland was set beside Laud's policy in Scotland of the enforcement of ecclesiastical uniformity by armed force, and of a resumption of Church lands alienated to the nobility at the Reformation, it was clear to many English gentry that the writing was on the wall. Their political rights were threatened by the cessation of Parliament, and the interference of the Privy Council in the workings of the benches of Justices; their finances were threatened by arbitrary taxation based on long-forgotten medieval precedents; their title to property was threatened by the Commission for Defective Titles, the revival of the Forest Laws and the assumed danger of a resumption of Church property; their religion was threatened by a pro-Catholic foreign policy, the apparent spread of popery in England, and Laud's liturgical and sacramental changes in Church worship; their law – the common law which protected property rights – was threatened by Strafford's policy in Ireland and by the independent operations of the prerogative courts in England; their social status was threatened by the attempted elevation of the peerage as a separate privileged caste. It is hardly surprising that there were a lot of frightened and angry gentlemen in England in 1640.

It should be emphasized that it is only within the insular context of Whiggish English historiography that Charles's policy can be labelled reactionary and anachronistic rather than progressive. Seen from the continent of Europe, the objectives and methods of Charles, Laud and Strafford were precisely those in which the future lay. The strengthening of the links of Church and State, the suppression of dissidents on all fronts, the creation of an overwhelmingly powerful Court, the acquisition of extensive financial and military powers — these were the basis of the all-but-universal growth of royal absolutism in Europe. If the trend of the times led anywhere, it was in the direction marked out by Charles and his advisers.

This may explain what at first sight seems an anomaly, namely that the dissident Parliamentary leaders, both at Westminster and in the only two counties where it has been tested, were significantly older, by a medium of about ten years, than the loyal cavaliers. The median age difference in the House of Lords was only about two years, but of those peers under thirty-two years who took sides in the war, four out of five were Royalists and only one out of five Parliamentarians. In the Lower House, M.P.s in their twenties were Royalist rather than Parliamentarian in 1642 by a factor of 2 to 1; M.P.s in their fifties were Parliamentarians rather than Royalist by a factor of 2 to 1. This was more important politically than it would be today, since the high adult mortality of the period meant that young men obtained positions of responsibility very much earlier in their careers. Thus in 1640 about half the M.P.s were under the age of forty – a proportion higher than that for any subsequent Parliament in English history.[180] The most plausible explanation of this generation gap in reverse is that for men to be driven to revolution they needed to have had personal experience first of the corruption of Buckingham in the 1620s and then of the tyranny of Charles, Laud and Strafford in the 1630s. If both experiences were necessary, but neither by itself was sufficient, this would explain both why the Revolution did not occur in the 1620s and why the old were more radical than the young in the 1640s. The unexpected conservatism of the young is still puzzling. It may be, however, that changes in the universities had created among the dons an intellectual climate favourable to Royalist and high Anglican ideas, which were now beginning to take hold of some of the new generation coming out of Oxford and Cambridge.[181] If this is so, time was on Charles's side, and he was undone by his own impetuous folly in provoking a show-down with the Scots while frightening his subjects with hints of popery and threats of tyranny.

It is thus just possible that a personally more charismatic king, with an irreproachably Protestant reputation and more cautious and far-sighted advisers, might have continued for quite a long time to pursue rather similar policies, at a much slower pace and using much greater tact, without running into serious trouble. On the other hand, nothing could compensate for the lack of a local bureaucracy, religious unity, a standing army, and some independent supply of money. The consequent relative impotence of Charles and Laud to enforce their policies is revealed by the failure of their attempts to revive the Crown's authority over the forests, to extract the full amount of ship money year after year, to stop privateering and interloping in the Caribbean, to censor the press, or to silence the Puritan preachers in London. In the long run Charles and Laud were thwarted on every major issue, and when faced with open military defiance from the Scots they had to back down. The necessary military and financial aid could only come from one of the Catholic powers, help from which would immediately alienate almost all the propertied classes, as James II was to discover to his cost. Thus in the long run the traditional view is correct, and Charles's policy was as doomed to failure as was that of his son half a century later. Given these conditions it seems legitimate to continue to describe royal policies in the 1630s as both reactionary and unrealistic.

The result of one hundred years of complex social, economic, religious, administrative and political change was to create a society that was evidently coming apart at the seams. Polarization was developing everywhere: between the rich and the not so rich, the countryside and the City, the Country and the Court, each county and all others, the bishops and the lower clergy, the clergy and the laity, the Puritans and the Arminians, the nobles and the gentry, the common lawyers and the Civil lawyers and prerogative court officials, the monopoly merchants and the lesser traders, the aldermen and the common councillors. In the 1630s internal tensions were rising on all sides, and the sense of national cohesion was weakening under the strain of so many hatreds and jealousies.

The three theoretical propositions upon which the foregoing argument is based are that deprivation is relative not absolute, and has to be measured against some identified reference group; that deprivation leads to frustration, which often can find relief only in aggression; and that this aggression is frequently directed not against the true source of the trouble but against a scapegoat. The scapegoat is primarily identified not by its economic but by its cultural distinctiveness, and in this case the two scapegoats for the many frustrated social groups were the papists and the courtiers, who were regarded as the embodiments of all evil. Since the King and his advisers were clearly associate with the Court and were widely believed to be popishly inclined, a situation had arisen by 1639 in which the popular scapegoat was not a powerless minority group but was the government itself. No state can long survive under such circumstances.

4. The triggers, 1640-2

The precipitants of the 1630s turned the prospects of political break-down from a possibility to a probability. But it was a sequence of short-term, even fortuitous, events which turned the probability into a certainty. Chalmers Johnson has observed that 'revolution is always avoidable if only the creative potentialities of political organization can be realized.'[182] Those potentialities were never even noticed by the King and his advisers in the years 1639–42. The governmental collapse of 1640 followed directly from the decision of Laud and Charles to try to impose on the Scottish clergy the English system of worship and Church organization at the same time as they threatened the Scottish noblemen with the loss of their ex-monastic estates. This drove the Presbyterian ministers and the nobility into an alliance, and provoked a full-scale war. Defeat in the war, caused largely by the unwillingness of the English troops and their leaders to fight, in turn led to the loss by the Crown of control over its armed forces, which is the first and most necessary prelude to revolution. The partial tax-payers' strike, the cost of the war, and the reparations demanded by the Scots combined to empty the royal treasury and led to financial collapse. Denied financial aid by the City of.London, the government could only raise the cash to carry on by an appeal to Parliament, which meant surrender to the now fully-aroused forces of opposition to all aspects of royal policy. Military defeat and financial bankruptcy are the two necessary preludes to a 'Great Revolution', as the histories of the English, French and Russian Revolutions show. By the autumn of 1640 the folly, obstinacy and misjudgment of Charles and Laud had brought the English government to its knees. Just as the authoritarian plans of Olivarez for Spain were defeated by rebellions in the dependent areas of Catalonia and Portugal, so were the authoritarian plans of 'Thorough' for England defeated by rebellions in the dependent areas, first Scotland and then Ireland.

The Parliamentary election of 1640 was more bitterly and widely contested than any that had gone before it, and the supporters of the Court everywhere went down in defeat. Courtiers, officials and hangers-on comprised 28 per cent of the Parliament of 1614 but only

11 per cent of the Long Parliament, a smaller proportion than in any previous Parliament of which we have record. Moreover, not only were many official candidates rejected, but the old aristocratic patronage system showed signs of breaking down for all but the most resolute and popular opposition leaders, like Warwick. The Earl of Salisbury could no longer get his nominee into even one seat at St Albans, and Lord Maynard was frustrated in Essex, although both were to side with Parliament. The latter complained furiously – and ominously – that 'fellows without shirts challenge as good a voice as myself.'[183]

For the Short Parliament of 1640, this process of erosion of the old aristocratic and Court electoral influence can be documented with some precision. Royalist peers nominated 78 men as candidates, only 49 of whom were elected (19 of those elected were not clear royalists). By way of contrast, all 24 candidates nominated by opposition peers were returned. The humiliation of the Court itself was even greater. Judging from past experience, the various conciliar agencies of the Crown should have been able to influence 78 elections, but they judged it prudent to interfere in only 47. Including efforts made elsewhere, the Court agencies nominated 66 candidates, all but 14 of whom were defeated. A more crushing demonstration of the collapse of royal authority before an aroused electorate could hardly be imagined. Equally significant is the fact that, perhaps for the first time in English history, this election centred around national politics as much as particular personalities, so that men could campaign on slogans such as 'Choose no ship (money) sheriff, no Court atheist, no fen drainer, nor church papist.' Of the issues raised, those of religion and arbitrary taxation predominated.[184]

When the Long Parliament met in 1640, Charles found himself almost alone. Of his natural allies, the aristocracy was weakened by decades of first economic and then status decline, and was deeply divided in its religious and political loyalties, a significant minority openly siding with his enemies; the Church hierarchy was isolated, despised, and almost as seriously split between supporters and opponents of Laudianism; the central administration was demoralized and untrustworthy; many courtiers were quietly leaving the sinking ship; the armed forces were shattered by defeat, and if forced to choose many were liable to side with the opposition, or even the Scots. Allied against the King was a temporarily united band of enemies – gentry, nobles, lawyers and ministers – inspired by four powerful but hitherto distinct, or even antagonistic, ideals: jingoistic nationalism, local particularism, religious and moral Puritanism, and constitutional legalism. They arrived at Westminster full of talk of a Reformed Church, a Godly Commonwealth, Magna Carta, the Ancient Constitution, and the Country. But these were slogans rather than a concrete programme, and it would be foolish to suggest that the opposition in 1640 had much more in mind than a desire to preserve and increase the political influence of Parliament, to establish the supremacy of the common law as a bulwark of property, to rid the Church of the popish innovations introduced by Laud, to put domestic and foreign policy on a forthrightly Protestant track, and to reduce the political influence of the bishops. But to achieve these objectives they had to tear down institutions like the prerogative courts, which were over 150 years old, to arrogate to themselves the power of determining the term of their own dissolution, to execute one leading minister of the Crown and drive another into exile, and to throw the Archbishop of Canterbury into the Tower.

By the summer of 1641 the united opposition had achieved all its negative objectives. It had removed from the Crown the powers of taxation without consent, and of arrest without trial; it had abolished the main organs of central government, the Councils of Wales and the North, the Courts of High Commission, Requests and Star Chamber; it had reversed the Laudian clerical and High Church policies and had stopped the persecution of dissenters; and it had punished the chief agents of royal policies. The first session of the Long Parliament had effectively destroyed or weakened all the central institutions of government except the common law courts, leaving power to slide comfortably into the hands of local authorities. This vacuum at the centre had at least two momentous consequences, the ending of censorship of the Press, which released a torrent of pamphlets and newspapers, and the ending of controls on religious worship, which gave rise to virtual religious anarchy. As yet, however, no one thought in terms of civil war, if only because the King had no one to fight for him except a handful of extremist Cavaliers. What changed the situation, and made war first possible and then inevitable, was a series of unfortunate accidents and misguided personal decisions.

Tension was enormously increased by two chance events, of which the first was the death of the Earl of Bedford, who at one time seemed likely to emerge as the leader of a moderate coalition government which would be acceptable both to the King and to the Parliamentary radicals. The second, which was far more serious, was the outbreak of the Irish Rebellion in November 1641. This was a violent and bloody mass uprising of Anglo-Catholic landlords and peasants against the recent English protestant settlers and the authoritarian .administration of Strafford. With hindsight one can see that the Irish situation had been becoming more and more explosive for a decade, but to contemporaries the rebellion, with its accompanying massacres and the loss of all English control outside the port towns, came like a bolt from the blue. Its timing could not have been more unfortunate, since the plain need to crush it made necessary the resurrection of central power in its most extreme and dangerous form, an army. Ever since the collapse of the government in 1640, there had been a vacuum of power, a situation which, had it not been for the Irish Rebellion, might have been allowed to continue for some time until the political crisis had been settled. But now there arose the necessity of raising an army, and therefore the question of who was to control it.

It was at this point that personal factors came to play a decisive part, in particular the bottomless duplicity of King Charles, whose actions, and whose intercepted correspondence, made it clear that he had no intention of accepting the new political order. In the summer of 1641 he visited Scotland in the vain hope of buying Scottish support against Parliament by judicious concessions over Presbyterianism and local patronage. From October 1641 he was clearly plotting a military *coup*, and the appointment of,the ruffianly Colonel Lunsford as Lieutenant of the Tower of London in late December was the prelude to the unsuccessful attempt to arrest the five leading members of the Parliamentary opposition on 4 January 1642.

The proven untrustworthiness of the King inevitably forced Pym and his allies to increase their demands, out of sheer necessity of self-preservation. They now genuinely feared for their lives: after all, it was they who had spilt the first blood – that of Strafford on the scaffold – and they knew that Charles had sworn revenge. They were therefore obliged, both for their personal safety and to protect the constitutional gains that they had won over the previous eighteen months, to demand control over the armed forces and control over the appointment of ministers. But these were demands that went far beyond the limited objective of restoring the old balanced constitution, and had truly revolutionary implications. The emergence of a strong party in the House of Commons with demands for the total abolition of episcopacy was further evidence of a swing to the left.

Part symptom and part cause of the deterioration in the situation was the increasingly radical rhetoric of the Puritan preachers, who were busy arousing the members of the Commons to a mood of high religious exaltation that could easily lead directly to bloodshed. In December 1641 Parliament had petitioned the King to institute a series of nation-wide public fasts on the last Wednesday of each month, so long as the Irish Rebellion continued. On the 8 January 1642 Charles committed the major blunder of agreeing with this request, and in doing so gave his enemies an ideal monthly platform. The key development was the adoption by the House of Commons of a policy of setting aside these Wednesdays as days of fasting and listening to sermons by preachers chosen by themselves. Many of these sermons, most of which were naturally of a Puritan persuasion, were subsequently printed and so reached a wider audience. The sermons played a critically important role, not so much in influencing policy on day-to-day business as in setting the ideological tone. The preachers offered members a frame of reference and a vision of men and affairs by which they could direct their thoughts and comprehend the bewildering experiences they were undergoing. The contents of these sermons thus fulfilled all the functions normally ascribed to an ideology.[185] They were cathartic, displacing frustrations and anxieties on to some specified scapegoat, first Catholics, then Cavaliers, and finally that 'man of blood', King Charles himself. They were morale-building, offering both an explanation of defeat in God's punishment of the nation for its sins, and a hope of victory in God's provident oversight of his Chosen People. They were unifying, in the mere fact of the collective ritual of fasting and attendance at St Margaret's Church to hear the sermons. And finally they were advocatory, in the sense that they articulated tensions, polarized thinking, and offered a vision of a reformed Church and Commonwealth in a holy Utopia of the not-too-distant future. It would be hard to exaggerate their significance over the seven years from 1642 to 1649.

Their role in creating the mood of the times is well illustrated by Stephen Marshall's famous and much quoted sermon, *Meroz Cursed*, delivered before the Commons on 23 February 1642. In it he bitterly denounced all waverers and neutralists, and called for wholehearted support of the Puritan cause. He interpreted the biblical text 'Cursed is everyone that withholdeth his hand from shedding blood' to mean encouragement to his hearers 'to go and embrue his hands in the blood of men, to spill and pour out the blood of women and children, like water in every street.' He told them that 'He is a blessed man that takes and dashes the little ones against the stones'.[186] His prospective victims were Irish, but it would clearly be not too great a step to divert this fanatical hatred towards any opposition group, whether English Protestant Royalists or Irish Catholic rebels. Once aroused, emotions of this intensity are hard to direct and control. The emergence in sermon literature of the Curse of Meroz as a biblical theme is a good indicator of rising internal tensions, and it is no accident that it became as prominent in the attacks of the American colonists on the neutrals and the Loyalist supporters of George III as it had been a hundred and thirty years before in the attacks of the English Parliamentarians on the neutrals and the Cavalier supporters of Charles I.[187]

This hardening of the opposition in the last months of 1641 was greatly stimulated by a political revolution in the city of London. Up to September the Mayor and Aldermen had remained fairly loyal to the King, and in November Charles could still claim, without too obvious falsification of the truth, that 'all those former tumults and disorders have only arisen from the meaner sorts of people, and that the affections of the better and main part of the City have ever been loyal and affectionate to my person and government.'[188] In December, however, skilful ward organization by the Parliamentary leaders, assisted by the London preachers, succeeded in giving the radicals victory in the elections to the Common Council. In January the Council set up a Committee of Public Safety—the first occasion of the appearance on the stage of history of such a body – whose function was to control the city militia, thus effectively bypassing the Mayor and Aldermen. The Parliamentary leaders now enjoyed the military protection of the armed forces of the city, the political assistance in critical moments of the mobs of the city, the financial backing of the wealth of the city, and the propaganda support of the preachers of the city. The price they had to pay, however, was the adoption of more radical policies than Pym at least would have wished to follow, given a free choice. With the political revolution in London, the outbreak of civil war came a large step nearer.

It takes two to make a fight, and what turned the threat of civil war into actuality was the formation of a strong Royalist party. Until the summer of 1641 Charles was virtually helpless, since his only reliable supporters were an unrepresentative minority of ultras. From then onwards, however, it is possible to watch a slow drift of the moderates away from Parliament and back to the King. The voting in the House of Commons tells its own tale. In May 1641, the motion to attaint Strafford carried by 204 to 59. In November the motion for control over the armed forces carried by 151 to 110. In the same month the Grand Remonstrance, that disingenuous propaganda blast against a decade of royal misgovernment and broken promises, squeaked through by 159 to 148. In June 1642 302 members stayed with Parliament on the outbreak of war, and 236 left London, mostly to join the King at York. Thus in a little over a year the number of Royalist members of Parliament had risen from 59 to 236.[189] As the M.P.s moved, so moved large numbers of country gentry.

This conversion of moderate reformers in 1640 into reluctant Royalists in 1642 is not difficult to understand. They were reacting against the political radicalism of Pym's demands for control over the armed forces and over the appointment of ministers, and against the religious radicalism of schemes to abolish episcopacy and extend the boundaries of toleration. They were also reacting, as members of the propertied classes, against the threats to law and order: to the enclosure riots and the non-payment of rents in the countryside; to the mobs which surged around the House at moments of crisis; to the wilder excesses of a totally unrestrained press; and to the emergence of a host of weird religious sects.

In August 1642 the local authorities in every town and county were forced to make a choice, for they were faced with two incompatible demands: for the implementation of a Militia Ordinance from Parliament to raise troops 'to defend the King' – meaning to attack him; and for the implementation of a Commission of Array from the King to raise troops to defend him – meaning to attack Parliament. 'The great quarrel between the king and us was the militia', reminisced Ludlow seventeen years later, and it was indeed on this issue that the civil war began.[190] There can be no doubt that the great majority of the propertied classes viewed the war with horror and apprehension. Very many contrived to stay neutral, and of those who fought there were substantial numbers who were as afraid of victory as of defeat, and who hoped for a stalemate. There were plenty of Royalists who were afraid of what the King would do if he won an outright military victory, and there were many Parliamentarians who saw no point in a crushing military defeat of the King, and who preferred a policy of regulated application of force to bring about a compromise political settlement. But, as so often happens, on both sides it was the radical tail which wagged the moderate dog. The combination of the City, those of the gentry who stayed with the

Parliamentary leaders and a substantial minority of powerful noblemen like Warwick, Northumberland, Essex and Salisbury was now strong enough to oppose the King by force of arms. But the composition of the alliance inevitably threw the weight on influence in the direction of the more radical wing in the City and in the House of Commons, while Pym's death in the middle of the war opened the way to more extremist leadership.

It must be remembered that mass political participation had its theoretical justification in pre-war Puritan thinking. It was Hanserd Knollys who in 1641 told his audience: 'You that are of the meaner rank, common people, be not discouraged: for God intends to make use of the common people in the great work of proclaiming the kingdom of his son.' These ideas, and the necessity of securing new allies on the left, led the Parliamentary leaders, who were by nature fairly conservative men of property, to support an increase in popular participation in the political process, which in more normal times they would have regarded with suspicion. Revolutions make strange bedfellows, and generate strange ideas. To illustrate this radicalizing process at work, one example will suffice. In April 1643 there was an election of church-wardens at St Dunstan's-in-the-East, in the city of London which was confined, as usual, to the closed circle of select vestrymen. But 'the major part of the inhabitants meeting in the same church, and conceiving the choice of vestrymen concerning the choosing of church-wardens without the consent of the rest of the inhabitants to be illegal, although customary,' declared the election void and appealed to Parliament for judgment. A Commons Committee supported the popular vote, which promptly chose a slate of Puritan supporters of the war.[191] Thus democracy triumphed over élitism with the active encouragement of the gentry in Parliament, who found themselves obliged to seek popular support in the prosecution of the war. Similarly on the Royalist side, although it was the shift of the more conservative gentry back to the King which gave him the army and the political support he needed, it was nevertheless the extreme Cavaliers who continued to exert the greatest influence over royal policies. Charles persisted in turning for advice to his more headstrong and intemperate advisers like Prince Rupert and Queen Henrietta Maria, rather than to the more cautious and conciliatory Sir Edward Hyde. Thus civil war began, and continued, since the respective demands had become non-negotiable to increasingly powerful elements in the leadership of both sides.

Despite the prodigious amount of research devoted to the subject

in recent years, the motives for the alignments of the gentry when
the war began are still not wholly clear. Everything points to the fact
that right up to the last minute a great majority of the gentry were
anxious to avoid armed conflict, and that very substantial numbers
contrived to stay neutral throughout its course. In Yorkshire 240
out of the total 680 gentry in the county never committed themselves
to either side. Neither a study of the M.P.s themselves, nor local
studies of the county gentry, have succeeded in showing any clear
association of wealth with political sympathies in 1642, although such
a correlation does appear after 1645. The theory that the Parliamentarians were 'mere gentry' as opposed to the court-connected
Royalists is not supported by the available facts. Nor has the theory
that the Parliamentarians were men of declining fortunes embittered
by economic decay fared any better. In Yorkshire, of those gentry
families who appear to have been in financial decay and who took
sides, three quarters threw in their lot with the King and only one
quarter with Parliament.[192] A more plausible hypothesis is that men
of declining fortunes tended to join the Royalists in the hopes of
recouping through army pay, plunder and the confiscation of rebel
estates. This was certainly the excuse offered by many Royalists
after the war, when it came to compounding for their delinquency.
Henry Cromwell 'being much indebted, went into the King's
quarters and bore arms'; Robert West 'was obliged by his debts . . .
to leave his dwelling and repair to the King's garrison'.[193]

Far more decisive than any socio-economic correlations is that
with religion. In Yorkshire over one third of the Royalist gentry
were Catholics, and over a half of the Parliamentarians were Puritans.
To put it another way, of those who took sides, 90 per cent of all
Catholics became Royalists, and 72 per cent of all Puritans became
Parliamentarians. *All* the Parliamentary leaders in Yorkshire had a
previous record of strong Puritan sympathies. There is reason to
think that those who had opposed the Crown on purely constitutional and political grounds in the 1620s and 1630s tended to swing
back to the King with Sir Edward Hyde in 1642, while those who had
also opposed the Crown on religious grounds were far more likely to
stick to Pym and fight for the Parliamentary cause. Finally there is
that fact that the Parliamentarians were on the average older than
the Royalists by about ten years.

Among the peerage, the most striking thing is how many of a
status group whose fortunes were so closely bound up with those of
monarchy, none the less either fought against the King or stayed on

the sidelines and avoided taking sides. This is important evidence of a serious decline of confidence among the nobles, both in their own order and in the monarchy which supported it. Among the substantial minority of 25 per cent who sided with Parliament, and so gave the cause its essential elements of patronage and respectibility, there were relatively few new men or small men. Only one came from a family in economic decline over the previous forty years, and the majority were from active, enterprising, and economically advancing families.[194] Essex, Northumberland, and Pembroke came from well-established peerage lines, and both they and Salisbury were some of the richest and most influential men in England. Some, like Northumberland, were disaffected courtiers who hated the policies and personalities of 'Thorough'; others, like Essex, had personal grudges to pay off against the Crown; many, like Saye and Sele and Brooke, had earlier shown proof of strong Puritan religious convictions. What they all had in common was a sympathy to religious reform, and a traditional, medieval hostility to royal constitutional autocracy.

When it came, the civil war did not merely fissure the landed classes right down the middle, it also split families apart, father against son and brother against brother: one in every seven peerage families was fragmented by war. Some contemporary cynics argued that these family divisions were part of a carefully arranged insurance policy, so that whichever side won there would always be someone with influence among the victors to protect the family property from confiscation and dismemberment.[195] But the bitterness so often engendered by these family divisions makes it clear that in many cases, if not in all, they derived from genuine differences of opinion over the political and religious issues at stake in the war.[196]

In the towns, leadership was in the hands of a limited group of families who dominated both the Courts of Aldermen and the main trading companies, and who owed their hereditary grip on political power and economic privilege to royal charter and royal support. They were therefore normally either openly Royalist or cautiously neutral, since their main precocupations were first, to preserve their positions, and second, to save their cities from the horrors of a siege and a sack at the hands of the armies of either side.

But other important merchant elements can now be identified, men interested especially in the American trades, in New England colonization, and in breaking the monopoly of the East India and Levant Companies. They were new men in new fields of entrepreneurial endeavour who chafed at the political and economic stranglehold of the older established monopolistic oligarchies. They were usually Puritan in their religious opinions, they wanted to reorient English foreign policy and commercial policy to a more aggressive and dynamic thrust towards the Americas, and they wanted to open up the Mediterranean and Indian trade to new-comers.[197] These men were important members of the group of radicals who seized control of London at a critical moment in 1641, and so swung the power and influence of the city decisively on the side of Parliament. On the other hand, they had little except a leavening of Puritanism, an interest in American trade and settle-ment and a common enemy in the monopolistic Crown to bind them to the grandees of the Country.

Further down the social scale, the small merchants, tradesmen, shop-keepers, artisans and apprentices tended to be Puritan in sympathy and Parliamentarian in allegiance, with a view to breaking the ramparts of privilege which protected the entrenched oligarchy. In so far as these groups were able to seize power, which they did in London and Newcastle, they turned the resources of their city over to the Parliamentary forces. This action in London was of decisive importance in tipping the scales against the Royalists in terms of troops and money, and it was the realization of this fact which drove the exasperated Royalists to such inspired heights of partisan vitu-peration: 'If, therefore, posterity shall ask . . . who could have pulled the Crown from the king's head, taken the government off its hinges, dissolved monarchy, enslaved the laws, and ruined the country – say "twas the proud, unthankful, schismatic, rebellious City of London." '[198]

Since the labouring poor, both rural and urban, played no part whatever in the Revolution except as cannon-fodder for both sides, it was the clash of these elements among the propertied and near-propertied classes, together with their necessary intellectual allies, the Puritan clergy and the common lawyers, which dictated the outcome of the war.

5. Conclusion

This essay is not concerned with the causes of the further stages of the Revolution. The war began with a fissuring of the traditional élites, but there followed the capture of the Parliamentary leadership by the hardline proponents of military victory, the emergence of a genuinely radical lower-middle-class social and political programme and party in the Levellers, the destruction of the three old landmarks, Monarchy, House of Lords and Episcopal Church, the replacement of the Commonwealth by a barely disguised military dictatorship, and the final collapse of the revolutionary regime and the restoration of the old order in 1660. The scope of this essay is limited to defining the long-term factors which made some modifications of the political and religious institutions very probable; the short-term factors, mainly errors of policy, which made it likely that the change would take the form of confrontation rather than adjustment; and the immediate events and decisions which caused first the central government to collapse, and then the victors to fall out over fundamentals, so that the country drifted unhappily into war two years later.

To make sense of these events, to explain in a coherent way why things happened the way they did, has necessitated the construction of multiple helix chains of causation more complicated than those of DNA itself. The processes of society are more subtle than those of nature. It has not proved possible – indeed it is patently quite impossible – to identify any one cause and label it the decisive, or even the most important one of all. Even the decision of Charles I in 1629 to embark on a strong policy of law and order in Church and State, though clearly critical in leading up to a breakdown, was itself no more than one step in a long anterior chain, an almost Pavlovian response to previous aggressions by the Parliamentary opposition, the ultimate causes of which have to be traced far back into the early Tudor period. The explanation of the English Revolution offered here is orderly, perhaps too orderly, but it is neither simple nor neat.

What was important about the English Revolution was not its success in permanently changing the face of England – for this was slight – but the intellectual content of the various opposition programmes and achievements after 1640. For the first time in history an anointed king was brought to trial for breach of faith with his subjects, his head was publicly cut off, and his office was declared abolished. An established church was abolished, its property was seized, and fairly wide religious toleration for all forms of Protestantism was proclaimed and even enforced. For a short time, and perhaps for the first time, there came on to the stage of history a group of men proclaiming ideas of liberty not liberties, equality not privilege, fraternity not deference. These were ideas that were to live on, and to revive again in other societies in other ages. In 1647 the Puritan John Davenport forecast correctly that 'the light which is now discovered in England . . . will never be wholly put out, though I suspect that contrary opinions will prevail for a time.'[199]

Although the Revolution ostensibly failed, although Monarchy, Lords, and Anglican Church were restored, although reforms of the electoral system, the law, the administration, the Church and the educational system were completely blocked for nearly two hundred years, although the social structure became a good deal more hierarchical and immobile after the Revolution than it was before, something nevertheless survived. There survived ideas about religious toleration, about limitations on the power of the central executive to interfere with the personal liberty of the propertied classes, and about a polity based on the consent of a broad spectrum of society. These ideas reappear in the writings of John Locke, and find expression in the political system in the reigns of William III and Anne. Its features were a very large and vocal electorate, well-developed party organizations, and the transfer of far-reaching powers to Parliament. A Bill of Rights, a Toleration Act and an annual Mutiny Act effectively restrained the repressive powers of the executive, and, together with further gains won by the common law judges, made the personal and political liberties of the English propertied classes the envy of eighteenth-century Europe. These benefits were not extended to the poor, who remained at the mercy of their social superiors, but the establishment of these ideas as the common property of the political nation was something quite new. It was something which prepared the way for the extension of these privileges down the social scale at a later date, and something which could serve as a model in other times and places.[200] It is this legacy of ideas which makes it reasonable to claim that the crisis in England in the seventeenth century is the first 'Great Revolution' in the history of the world, and therefore an event of fundamental importance in the evolution of Western civilization.

Notes

The notes to this chapter are intended to draw attention to the very great body of research which has been published over the last twenty years and upon which so much of the argument is based. Facts which have long been familiar and are in all the textbooks are not footnoted.

1 E. Hyde, Earl of Clarendon, *The History of the Rebellion and Civil Wars in England*, ed. W. D. Murray, Oxford, 1888.

2 C. V. Wedgwood, *The King's Peace, 1637–41*, London, 1955.

3 S. R. Gardiner, *The First Two Stuarts and the Puritan Revolution*, London, 1876.

4 T. B. Macaulay, *The History of England from the Accession of James II*, London, 1849; G. M. Trevelyan, *England Under the Stuarts*, London, 1925.

5 F. Engels, *Socialism: Utopian and Scientific*, London, 1892, pp. xix–xxiv; C. Hill, *The English Revolution, 1640*, London, 1940, pp. 9–82; R. H. Tawney, 'The rise of the gentry, 1558–1640', *Economic History Review*, 11, 1941; 'Harrington's interpretation of his Age', *Proceedings of the British Academy*, 27, 1941. M. Dobb, *Studies in the Development of Capitalism*, London, 1946, pp. 109–51, 161–76, 186–220, 224–39. For a neo-Marxist interpretation, see Barrington Moore Jnr, *Social Origins of Dictatorship and Democracy*, Boston, 1966, Part I, ch. 1. For a modified Marxist interpretation allowing a greater role to religion and ideas, see C. Hill, 'La Révolution anglaise du XVIIe siècle', *Revue Historique*, 221, 1959, and his *Century of Revolution, 1603–1714*, London, 1961. For a savage onslaught on these theories, see J. H. Hexter, 'The myth of the middle class in Tudor England', in his *Reappraisals in History*, London, 1961.

6 C. E. Black, *The Dynamics of Modernization*, New York, 1966, pp. 72–4, 90, 106–8

7 H. R. Trevor-Roper, 'The gentry, 1540–1640', *Economic History Review*, Supplement 1, 1953.

8 J. Harrington, *Oceana*, 1737, p. 70.

9 S. Neumann, 'The international Civil War', *World Politics*, 1, 1949, pp. 33–4, n. 1.

10 S. C. Lomas, *Letters and Speeches of Oliver Cromwell*, II, London, 1906, p. 342.

11 J. Thirsk, 'The sale of Royalist land during the Interregnum', *Economic History Review*, 2nd ser., 5, 1952; 'The Restoration land settlement', *Journal of Modern History*, 26, 1954; H. J. Habakkuk, 'Landowners and the Civil War', *Economic History Review*, 2nd ser., 18, 1965; 'The Parliamentary army and the Crown lands', *Welsh Historical Review*, 3, 1967.

12 S. R. Gardiner, *The Constitutional Documents of the Puritan Revolution, 1625–1660*, Oxford, 1906, p. 372.

13 *Catalogue of the Thomason Tracts in the British Museum, 1640–1661*, London, 1908, p. xxi. This collection is known to be far from complete.

14 W. M. Lamont, *Marginal Prynne, 1600–69*, London, 1963, p. 30.

15 C. Ogilvie, *The King's Government and the Common Law, 1471–1641*, Oxford, 1958; M. Judson, *The Crisis of the Constitution*, New Brunswick, 1949, ch. 2; C. Hill, *Intellectual Origins of the English Revolution*, Oxford, 1965, ch. 5; W. S. Holdsworth, *A History of English Law*, London, 1937, 5, pp. 425–93.

16 C. Hill, 'The Norman yoke', in his *Puritanism and Revolution*, London, 1958, Part I, ch. 3.

17 T. Hobbes, 'Human nature', *English Works*, ed. W. Molesworth, 1841, 4, p. 16.

18 J. F. Wilson, *Pulpit in Parliament: Puritanism during the English Civil Wars, 1640–1648*, Princeton, 1969; H. R. Trevor-Roper, 'The Fast Sermons of the Long Parliament', in his *Religion, the Reformation and Social Change*, London, 1967; J. C. Spalding, 'Sermons before Parliament (1640–49) as a Puritan Diary', *Church History*, 36, 1967.

19 C. Hill, *God's Englishman*, London, 1970, p. 55; *Historical MSS. Commission*, 2nd Report, p. 63; C. Hill, *Puritanism and Revolution*, op. cit., p. 124; J. T. Cliffe, *The Yorkshire Gentry from the Reformation to the Civil War*, London, 1969, p. 348.

20 M. Walzer, *The Revolution of the Saints*, Cambridge, Mass., 1965, pp. 10–11.

21 T. Hobbes, *De Cive*, 1651, quoted in P. Zagorin, *The Court and the Country*, London, 1969, p. 347; H. Parker, *Observations upon some of his Majesties later Answers and Expresses*, London, 1642; M. Judson, 'Henry Parker and the theory of Parliamentary sovereignty', in *Essays in History and Political Thought in Honor of C. H. McIlwain*, Cambridge, Mass., 1936.

22 *Cal. S. P. Venetian, 1647–52*, p. 129. I owe this reference to Mr R. Barahona.

23 G. E. Lenski, 'Status crystallization: a non-vertical dimension of social status', *American Sociological Review*, 19, 1954. See above, p. 19.

24 C. A. Holmes, 'The Eastern Association', Cambridge Ph.D. thesis, 1969, p. 90.

25 S. R. Gardiner, op. cit., 2, pp. 230–2, 277–9.

26 Based on a study of the biographies in M. F. Keeler, *The Long Parliament, 1640–41*, Philadelphia, 1954.

27 A. Everitt, *The Community of Kent and the Great Rebellion, 1640–60*, Leicester, 1966, pp. 143, 242.

28 For this and other objections, see C. Hill, 'Recent interpretations of the Civil War', in his *Puritanism and Revolution*; P. Zagorin, 'The social interpretation of the English Revolution', *Journal of Economic History*, 19, 1959; and J. H. Hexter, *Reappraisals in History*, op. cit., pp. 129–31.

29 F. Engels, op. cit.; R. H. Tawney, 'The Rise of the Gentry', op. cit., pp. 183–9, 203.

30 W. S. Robinson, 'Ecological correlations and the behaviour of individuals', *American Sociological Review*, 15, 1950.

31 D. M. Wolfe, *Leveller Manifestoes of the Puritan Revolution*, London, 1944, p. 237.

32 *Calendar of State Papers Spanish*, 1, p. 178.

33 Edward Lord Herbert, *The Life and Reign of King Henry VIII*, London, 1683, p. 4.

34 The liberal/constitutional view of Henry VIII and Cromwell was established in the early 1950s by G. R. Elton, and became the official orthodoxy with the publication of his *England Under the Tudors*, London, 1955. The first major attack on it came with J. H. Hurstfield, 'Was there a Tudor despotism after all?', *Transactions of the Royal Historical Society*, 5th ser., 17, 1967.

35 Both A. F. Pollard, *Henry VIII*, London, 1905, pp. 397–415, and R. B. Wernham, *Before the Armada: the Growth of English Foreign Policy*, London, 1966, chs. 12, 13, 14, have tried to fit the war into a grand strategy. The fallacies have been pointed out by J. J. Scarisbrick, op. cit., p. 424.

36 H. Miller, 'Subsidy assessments of the peerage in the sixteenth century', *Bulletin of the Institute of Historical Research*, 28, 1955; F. C. Dietz, 'English Government Finance, 1485–1558', *University of Illinois Studies in the Social Sciences*, 9, 1920, p. 94; J. Hurstfield, 'The profits of fiscal feudalism, 1541–1602', *Economic History Review*, 2nd ser., 8, 1955.

37 Church property in the West Riding of Yorkshire amounted to just over one quarter of the whole (R. B. Smith, *Land and Politics in the England of Henry VIII*, Oxford, 1970, p. 73).

38 Dietz, op. cit., chs. 10, 11, 12, 14.

39 M. B. Donald, *Elizabethan Copper*, London, 1955, chs. 6, 11.
E. Hughes, 'The English monopoly of salt in the years 1563–
1571', *English Historical Review*, 40, 1925; R. B. Turton, *The
Alum Farm*, Whitby, 1938.

40 G. Aylmer, *The King's Servants*, London, 1961, chs. 3, 4;
K. W. Swart, *Sale of Offices in the Seventeenth Century*, The
Hague, 1949, ch. 3.

41 F. C. Dietz, *English Public Finance, 1558–1641*, New York,
1932, pp. 235, 265–6, 303–4, 362–79, 391; L. Stone, *The Crisis
of the Aristocracy, 1558–1641*, Oxford, 1965, pp. 496–8.

42 L. Stone, 'The political programme of Thomas Cromwell',
Bulletin of the Institute for Historical Research, 24, 1951, pp. 4–
18; W. K. Jordan, *Edward VI: The Young King*, London,
1968, p. 466, n. 2.

43 Stone, *The Crisis of the Aristocracy*, op. cit., pp. 201–17; G. C.
Cruikshank, *Elizabeth's Army*, Oxford, 1966, chs. 1, 2; L.
Boynton, *The Elizabethan Militia, 1558–1638*, London, 1967,
chs. 1–4.

44 The most recent and balanced survey of this problem is E. W.
Ives, 'The common lawyers in Pre-Reformation England',
Transactions of the Royal Historical Society, 5th ser., 18, 1968,
pp. 162–73.

45 W. C. Richardson, *Tudor Chamber Administration, 1485–1547*,
Baton Rouge, 1952, pp. 433–42; G. R. Elton, *The Tudor
Revolution in Government*, Cambridge, 1953, pp. 223–4; 'The
Elizabethan exchequer: war in the receipt', in *Elizabethan
Government and Society*, ed. S. T. Bindoff *et al.*, London, 1961.

46 W. H. Dunham, Jr., 'Lord Hastings' indentured retainers',
Trans. Connecticut Acad. of Arts and Sciences, 39, 1955.

47 M. E. James, *Change and Continuity in the Tudor North: the
Rise of Thomas first Lord Wharton* (Borthwick papers 27),
York, 1965; *A Tudor Magnate and the Tudor State: Henry fifth
Earl of Northumberland* (Borthwick Papers 30), York, 1966;
'The first Earl of Cumberland and the decline of northern
feudalism', *Northern History*, 1, 1966.

48 For two good local studies, see W. B. Willcox, *Gloucestershire:
a Study in Local Government, 1590–1640*, New Haven, 1940;
T. G. Barnes, *Somerset, 1625–40*, London, 1961.

49 J. F. Williams, 'The married clergy of the Marian period',
Norfolk Archaeology, 32, 1958–61.

50 Quoted by P. Miller, *Orthodoxy in Massachussetts, 1630–50*,
Cambridge, Mass., 1933, p. 19.

51 W. T. MacCaffrey, 'England: the Crown and the new
aristocracy, 1540–1600', *Past and Present*, 30, 1965; Stone,

The Crisis of the Aristocracy, op. cit., p. 97; J. C. Youings, *Devon Monastic Lands, Devon and Cornwall Rec. Soc.*, New series, 1, 1955, pp. xx–xxi; G. Scott Thomson, *Two Centuries of Family History*, London, 1930, p. 166. '

52 S. B. Liljegren, *The Fall of the Monasteries and the Social Changes in England Leading up to the great Revolution*, Lund, 1924.

53 F. S. Siebert, *Freedom of the Press in England, 1476–1776*, Urbana, 1965, Parts 1 and 2; A. G. Dickens, *The English Reformation*, London, 1964, pp. 26–37, 68–82, 190–2, 264–79; P. Collinson, *The Elizabethan Puritan Movement*, London, 1967, pp. 48–55, 141–7, 432–47; 'John Field and Elizabethan Separatism', in *English Government and Society*; A. F. Allison and D. M. Rogers, *A Catalogue of Catholic Books in English Printed Abroad and Secretly in England, 1558–1640*, Bognor Regis, 1956, p. 176; H. S. Bennett, *English Books and Readers, 1558–1603*, Cambridge, 1965, pp. 74–86; op. cit., *1603–40*, Cambridge, 1970, pp. 89–90.

54 C. Hill, *The Economic Problems of the Church*, Oxford, 1956, ch. 4; E. Rosenberg, *Leicester; Patron of Letters*, New York, 1955, ch. 4.

55 S. E. Lehmberg, *The Reformation Parliament, 1529–36*, Cambridge, 1970. For an international comparison, see J. P. Cooper, 'Differences between English and Continental governments in the 17th century', in *Britain and the Netherlands*, 1, ed. J. S. Bromley and E. H. Kossman, London, 1960.

56 J. J. Scarisbrick, op. cit., plate 3.

57 J. E. Neale, *Elizabeth and her Parliaments*, 1, 2, London, 1953, 1957.

58 George Duke of Albemarle, *Observations on Political and Military Affairs*, London, 1671, p. 145.

59 J. Cornwall, 'English population in the early sixteenth century', *Economic History Review*, 2nd ser., 23, 1970; D. V. Glass and D. E. C. Eversley, *Population in History*, London, 1965, pp. 203–4; *V. C. H. Leicestershire*, 3, pp. 137–42; J. Thirsk, *The Agrarian History of England and Wales*, 4, Cambridge, 1967, pp. 593–609; I. Blanchard, 'Population change, enclosure, and the Early Tudor economy', *Economic History Review*, 2nd ser., 23, no. 3, 1970.

60 E. Kerridge, *The Agricultural Revolution*, London, 1967 (see the review by G. E. Mingay in *Agricultural History Review*, 17 (no. 2), 1969, pp. 151–4); W. G. Hoskins, 'Harvest fluctuations and English economic history, 1620–1759', *Agricultural History Review*, 16 (no. 1), 1968, pp. 25–8; R. Mousnier, *Fureurs paysannes*, Paris, 1967.

61 F. J. Fisher, 'Commercial trends and policy in sixteenth-century England', *Essays in Economic History*, 1, ed. E. M. Carus-Wilson, London, 1954; L. Stone, 'Elizabethan overseas trade', *Economic History Review*, 2nd ser., 2, 1949; F. J. Fisher, 'London's export trade in the early seventeenth century', *Economic History Review*, 2nd ser., 3, 1950; W. B. Stephens, 'The cloth exports of the provincial ports, 1600–1640', *Economic History Review*, 2nd ser., 22, 1969; B. Supple, *Commercial Crisis and Change in England, 1600–1642*, Cambridge, 1964; R. Davis, 'English foreign trade, 1660–1700', *Essays in Economic History*, op. cit., 2, 1962; R. Davis, *English Overseas Trade, 1500–1700*, London, 1971; J. Thirsk, op. cit., pp. 466–592.

62 E. Misseldon, *Free Trade*, London, 1622, p. 40.

63 J. Crofts, *Pack-horse, Waggon and Post*, London, 1967.

64 L. Stone, *The Crisis of the Aristocracy*, op. cit., pp. 528–32; J. G. van Dillen, *History of the Principal Public Banks*, The Hague, 1934, p. 95.

65 J. U. Nef, 'The progress of technology and the growth of large-scale industry in Great Britain, 1540–1640', E. M. Carus-Wilson, *Essays in Economic History*, 1. D. C. Coleman, 'Industrial growth and industrial revolutions', ibid., 3, 1962.

66 E. A. Wrigley, 'A simple model of London's importance in changing English society and economy, 1650–1750', *Past and Present*, 37, 1967; L. Stone, 'Social mobility in England, 1500–1700', *Past and Present*, 33, 1966, p. 31; J. Cornwall, 'English population in the early sixteenth century', *Economic History Review*, 2nd ser., 23, 1970; C. A. F. Meekings, *Dorset Hearth Tax Assessments, 1662–4*, Dorset Nat. Hist. and Archaeol. Soc., 1951, pp. 108–9; *Victoria County History: City of York*, London, 1961, p. 162. R. Howell, *Newcastle upon Tyne and the Puritan Revolution*, Oxford, 1967, p. 9; W. MacCaffrey, *Exeter, 1540–1640*, Cambridge, Mass., 1958, p. 12; B. Little, *The City and County of Bristol*, London, 1954, p. 327.

67 L. Stone, 'Elizabethan overseas trade', op. cit., p. 39; F. J. Fisher, 'London's export trade in the early seventeenth century', op. cit., p. 152; R. Davis, 'English foreign trade, 1660–1700', op. cit., pp. 270–1. (The percentages for 1700 were deduced by me from Professor Davis's figures.)

68 J. Thirsk, 'Industries in the countryside', *Essays in the Economic and Social History of Tudor and Stuart England*, ed. F. J. Fisher, Cambridge, 1961; A. J. and R. H. Tawney, 'An occupational census of the seventeenth century', *Economic History Review*, 5, 1934–5.

69 L. Stone, 'Social mobility in England', op. cit.

70 A. G. Dickens, *The English Reformation*, London, 1964, pp. 163–6; L. Stone, *The Crisis of the Aristocracy, 1558–1641*, op. cit., Apps. III, VI; J. Cornwall, 'The early Tudor gentry', *Economic History Review*, 2nd ser., 17, 1964–5, pp. 457–61; C. B. McPherson, *The Political Theory of Possessive Individualism*, Oxford, 1962, pp. 280–1.

71 B.M. Lansdowne MSS., 1218 f. 15; P.R.O., C. 193/12/3 ff. 44v–47.

72   *Sales of Crown Land*

Dates	Amount	Approximate Phelps-Brown Price Index (*)	Amount at 1630 Prices	Reference
1536–1554	£1,103,000	180	£3,677,000	F. C. Dietz, *English Government Finance 1485-1558*, Urbana, 1921, p. 217
1561–1563	176,000	300	352,000	S. J. Madge, *The Domesday of Crown Lands*, London, 1938, p. 41
1589–1603	641,000	480	801,000	op. cit., p. 42 (£817,000–176,000)
1603–1625	775,000	500	930,000	op. cit., p. 50
1625–1635	651,000	600	651,000	op. cit., p. 60
Total			£6,411,000	

* E. M. Phelps-Brown and S. V. Hopkins, 'Seven centuries of prices of consumables . . .' *Economica*, new ser., 23, 1956, p. 311.

73 To give but one example, when Sir William Cavendish bought four manors from the Crown for £6,300 in 1602, he spent several hundred pounds in bribes, including £100 to the Lord Treasurer, £50 to the Auditor of Rates for easy rating, £20 to the Attorney General to keep his mouth shut, and £10 to the latter's clerk – all over and above the normal fees. (Chatsworth House, Hardwick MSS., Drawer 143/40).

74 R. B. Smith, *Land and Politics in the England of Henry VIII*, op. cit., p. 218; J. Kerr, 'The disposal of Crown lands and the Devon Land market, 1536–58', *Agricultural History Review*, 18 (no. 1), 1970, pp. 95, 101.

75 L. Stone, *The Crisis of the Aristocracy*, op. cit., ch. 4.

76 References cited in L. Stone, 'Social mobility in England', op. cit., p. 26 n. 20, 21; O. Ashmore, 'Household inventories of Lancashire gentry, 1550–1700', *Lancs. and Cheshire Hist. Soc. Trans.*, 110, 1958; V. H. T. Skipp, 'Economic and social change in the Forest of Arden, 1530–1649', *Agricultural History Review*, 18, Supplement, 1970, pp. 101–5.

77 L. Stone, *The Crisis of the Aristocracy*, op. cit., pp. 257–68.

78 M. R. James, 'Obedience and dissent in Henrician England: The Lincolnshire Rebellion, 1536', *Past and Present*, 48, 1970, p. 70.

79 For a discussion of the debate on this issue see above, ch. 2, *passim.*

80 Stone, 'Social Mobility in England, 1500–1700', op. cit., p. 24.

81 Stone, op. cit., p. 27, n. 22; p. 19, n. 3; R. G. Howell, *Newcastle upon Tyne and the Puritan Revolution*, op. cit., ch. 2.

82 W. K. Jordan, *Edward VI: The Young King*, London, 1968, ch. 15.

83 It is now clear beyond all question that Professor Jordan exaggerated the importance of private charity in handling poor relief, and grossly underestimated the scope, scale and continuity of the tax-supported official system. The claim that 'the constructive effort, as well as most of the funds, flowed from private endowments rather than from the mechanism contemplated by legislation' is no longer tenable. (W. K. Jordan, *Philanthropy in England, 1480–1660*, London, 1959, pp. 18, 90, 107.) The evidence for the importance of organized public relief is assembled in A. L. Beier, 'Studies in Poverty and Poor Relief in Warwickshire, 1540–1680', Ph.D. thesis, Princeton University, 1969, p. 178. Mr Julian Hill informs me that his own researches in Shropshire confirm Dr Beier's findings.

84 C. S. L. Davies, 'Les Revoltes populaires en Angleterre (1500–1700)', *Annales*, 1969 (1); D. C. Allen, 'The Rising in the West, 1628–31', *Economic History Review*, 2nd ser., 6, 1952; E. Kerridge, 'The revolts in Wiltshire against Charles I', *Wilts. Arch. Mag.*, 57, 1958–9.

85 P. Zagorin, op. cit., p. 323; C. A. Holmes, op. cit., p. 93. For current attitudes see C. Hill 'The many-headed monster', in *From Renaissance to Counter-Reformation*, ed. C. H. Carter, New York, 1965.

86 W. L. Sachse, 'The mob and the Revolution of 1688', *Journal of British Studies*, 4 (no. 1), 1964.

87 J. Clapham, *Elizabeth of England*, ed. E. P. and C. Read, Philadelphia, 1951, pp. 27–8; G. Goodman, *The Court of King James I*, London, 1839, 2, p. 57.

88 B. Behrens, 'The Whig theory of the constitution in the reign of Charles II', *Cambridge Historical Journal*, 7, 1941–2, p. 44.

89 C. Falls, *Elizabeth's Irish Wars*, London, 1950, pp. 255, 258, 264, 277, 284, 324, 326, 329, 335, 341; Edmund Spenser, 'A View of the State of Ireland, in' *Ireland under Elizabeth and James I*, ed. H. Morley, London, 1890, pp. 143–4.

90 Dr P. Moynihan to President Nixon, *New York Times*, 11 March 1970, p. 30.

91 Stone, *The Crisis of the Aristocracy*, op. cit., pp. 405–11;
   F. D. Price, 'The abuses of excommunication and the decline
   of ecclesiastical discipline under Queen Elizabeth', *English
   Historical Review*, 57, 1942; W. Pierce, *Marprelate Tracts,
   1588, 1589*, London, 1911; Alexander Leighton, *Appeal to
   Parliament; or Sion's Plea against the Prelacie*, London, 1628.

92 Stone, op. cit., p. 406.

93 J. Selden, *Table Talk*, ed. F. Pollock, London, 1917, p. 17.

94 D. M. Barratt, 'The Condition of the Parish Clergy between
   the Reformation and 1660', D.Phil. thesis, Oxford, 1949, p. 9;
   J. I. Daeley, 'Pluralism during the administration of Matthew
   Parker', *Journal of Ecclesiastical History*, 18, 1967, p. 45;
   F. W. Brooks, 'The social position of the parson in the
   sixteenth century', *Journal of the British Archaeological
   Association*, 3rd ser., 10, 1945–7; W. G. Hoskins, 'The
   Leicestershire country parson in the sixteenth century', in
   his *Essays in Leicestershire History*, Liverpool, 1950; C. Hill,
   The Economic Problems of the Church, ch. 9; P. Tyler, 'The
   status of the Elizabethan parochial clergy', *Studies in Church
   History*, 4, 1967.

95 R. Howell, 'Puritanism in Newcastle before the summoning of
   the Long Parliament', *Archaeologia Aeliana*, 4th ser., 41, 1963,
   p. 138.

96 W. Perkins, *Foundations of the Christian Religion*, London,
   1595, sig. A2.

97 J. Hacket, *A Century of Sermons*, ed. T. Plume, London, 1675,
   p. xii.

98 J. Bossy, 'The character of Elizabethan Catholicism', *Past and
   Present*, 21, 1962; R. A. Marchant, *Religion and Society in
   Elizabethan Sussex*, Leicester, 1969, chs. 3, 8, 12.

99 P. Collinson, 'Episcopacy and reform', *Studies in Church
   History*, 3, 1966; *The Elizabethan Puritan Movement*, pp.
   191–207, 243–8, 432–67; I. Morgan, *The Godly Preachers of
   Elizabethan England*, London, 1965; P. Seaver, *The Puritan
   Lectureships*, Stanford, 1970; E. Rosenberg, op. cit., ch. 6;
   M. H. Curtis, 'Hampton Court Conference and its aftermath',
   History, 46, 1961; R. A. Marchant, op. cit., ch. 10.

100 C. Russell, 'Arguments for religious unity in England, 1530–
   1650', *Journal of Ecclesiastical History*, 18, 1967, p. 204;
   E. Lodge, *Illustrations of British History*, London, 1791, p. 260.

101 C. Russell, op. cit., p. 213; N. Ward, *To the High and
   Honorable Parliament of England*, London, 1648, p. 5;
   Dictionary of American Biography, 13, *sub.*, Urian J. Oakes.
   (I owe these references to Mr J. Pruett.)

102 The subsequent paragraphs about the aristocracy are a bald

summary of the arguments in Stone, *The Crisis of the Aristocracy*, op. cit., chs. 1, 3, 4, 10, 14.

103 For the role of the European court system, see H. R. Trevor-Roper, 'The general crisis of the 17th century', in *Crisis in Europe, 1560–1660*, ed. T. H. Aston, London, 1965. For the English Court, see Stone, *The Crisis of the Aristocracy*, op. cit., ch. 8; W. T. MacCaffrey, 'Place and patronage in Elizabethan politics', in *Elizabethan Government and Society*; G. V. P. Akrigg, *Jacobean Pageant*, Cambridge, Mass., 1962; J. H. Hexter, 'The English aristocracy, its crises, and the English Revolution, 1558–1660', *Journal of British Studies*, 8, 1968, pp. 57–69.

104 J. E. Neale, 'The Elizabethan political scene', in his *Essays in Elizabethan History*, London, 1958; L. Stone, 'The fruits of office: the case of Robert Cecil, 1st Earl of Salisbury, 1596–1612', *Essays in the Economic and Social History of Tudor and Stuart England*, ed. F. J. Fisher, London, 1961; J. P. Cooper, 'The fortune of Thomas Westworth, Earl of Strafford', *Economic History Review*, 2nd ser., 11, 1958; Stone, *The Crisis of the Aristocracy*, op. cit., pp. 100–6, 489–495; M. Prestwich, *Cranfield: Politics and Profits under the Early Stuarts*, Oxford, 1966, ch. 9; A. J. Loomie, 'Sir Robert Cecil and the Spanish Embassy', *Bulletin of the Institute of Historical Research*, 42, 1969.

105 J. Hurstfield, 'Corruption and reform under Edward VI and Mary', *English Historical Review*, 68, 1953.

106 G. R. Elton, 'Reform by statute: Thomas Starkey's *Dialogue* and Thomas Cromwell's policy', *Proceedings of the British Academy*, 54, 1968; W. G. Zeeveld, *Foundations of Tudor Policy*, London, 1948; W. K. Ferguson, *The Articulate Citizen and the English Renaissance*, Durham, N. C., 1965, pp. 361–80.

107 L. Stone, 'State control in sixteenth century England', *Economic History Review*, 17, 1947.

108 M. W. Beresford, 'The common informer, the penal statutes and economic regulation', *Economic History Review*, 2nd ser., 10, 1957; G. R. Elton, 'Informing for profit', in his *Star Chamber Stories*, London, 1958.

109 L. Stone, *The Crisis of the Aristocracy*, op. cit., pp. 426–49.

110 W. Tyndale, 'Obedience of a Christian Man', in *Doctrinal Treatises and Introduction to different Portions of the Holy Scriptures*, ed. H. Walter (Parker Soc.), 1848, pp. 177–8; A. G. Dickens, 'Royal Pardons for the Pilgrimage of Grace', *Yorkshire Archaeological Journal*, 33, 1938, p. 406; W. Haller, 'John Foxe and the Puritan Revolution', in R. F. Jones, *The Seventeenth Century*, Stanford, 1951, p. 209; W. Haller, *Foxe's Book of Martyrs and the Elect Nation*, London, 1963, p. 234.

111 E. C. Wilson, *England's Eliza*, Cambridge, Mass., 1939, pp. 33, 120, 215–22.

112 G. Goodman, *The Court of James the First*, London, 1839, 2, p. 379; N. E. McClure, *Letters of John Chamberlain*, Philadelphia, 1939, 2, p. 243; J. Harington, *Nugae Antiquae*, London, 1804, 1, pp. 348–53; F. Osborne, *Traditional Memoyres on the Raigne of Queen Elizabeth* in *Secret History of the Court of James I*, ed. W. Scott, Edinburgh, 1811, 1, p. 50; B.M. Harleian MSS., 6395, f. 50v. The importance of these stories lies in the fact of their existence, not in their truth. For other evidence of the widespread gossip about James's sexual tastes see F. Bamford, *A Royalist Notebook*, London, 1936, p. 196; J. Harington, op. cit., 1, pp. 391–5; E. Peyton, *Divine Catastrophe of the Kingly Family of the House of Stuarts*, in Scott, op. cit., 2, pp. 346, 348; F. Osborne, *Some Traditionall Memorialls on the Raigne of King James I*, in Scott, op. cit., 1, pp. 274–6; A. Weldon, *The Character of King James*, in Scott, op. cit., 1, p. 376; N. E. McClure, op. cit., 2, pp. 144; Bodl. Rawlinson MS., Poet, 26, f. 72v; Bodl. MS. Eng. Poet, C 50, f. 12.

113 D. H. Willson, *James VI and I*, London, 1956, chs. 20, 21; L. Stone, *The Crisis of the Aristocracy*, op. cit., pp. 662–71; W. B. Rye, *England as seen by Foreigners*, London, 1865, p. 229; S. A. Strong, *A Catalogue of Documents . . . at Welbeck*, London, 1903, p. 210. For examples of James's distaste for displaying himself to the public, see F. Bamford, *A Royalist Notebook*, op. cit., pp. 196–7; J. O. Halliwell, *Autobiography and Correspondence of Sir Simonds D'Ewes*, London, 1845, 1, p. 170.

114 Quoted by W. Haller 'John Foxe', p. 223; *Foxe's Book of Martyrs and the Elect Nation*, p. 241; and by P. Seaver, op. cit., p. 68. See also Edmund Calamy in 1642: 'God hath made us like Saul, taller by a head in mercies than all other Nations' (quoted by J. C. Spalding in *Church History*, 36, 1967, p. 31).

115 J. Hacket, *A Century of Sermons*, ed. J. Plume, London, 1675, p. xv.; L. Stone, *The Crisis of the Aristocracy, 1558–1641*, op. cit., pp. 388–9.

116 J. E. Neale, *The Elizabethan House of Commons*, London, 1949, chs. 7, 15.

117 M. Judson, *The Crisis of the Constitution*, New Brunswick, 1949, ch. 7; P. Zagorin, op. cit., ch. 7; W. M. Mitchell, *The Rise of a Revolutionary Party in the House of Commons, 1603–29*, New York, 1957, chp. 5; W. Notestein, *The Winning of the Initiative by the House of Commons*, London, 1924; J. R. Tanner, *Constitutional Conflicts of the 17th Century*,

London, 1928; F. D. Wormuth, *The Royal Prerogative, 1603–1649*, Ithaca, 1939.

118 *Declaration of the Causes moving the Queene to give aide to the People afflicted and oppressed in the low Countries*, London, 1585, sig. A1. *The Political Works of James I*, ed. C. H. McIlwain, Cambridge, Mass., 1918, p. 307.

119 R. B. Smith, *Land and Politics in the England of Henry VIII*, Oxford, 1970, ch. 4; J. Gleason, *The Justices of the Peace in England, 1558–1640*, Oxford, 1969, chs. 7, 8; T. Barnes, *Somerset, 1625–40*, London, 1961, chs. 3, 11. My awareness of the importance of this development has been heightened by many conversations with Mr Victor Morgan.

120 L. Stone, 'The educational revolution in England, 1560–1640', *Past and Present*, 28, 1966, pp. 54–64, 69; H. F. Kearney, *Scholars and Gentlemen*, London, 1970, chs. 3, 4; J. H. Plumb, *The Origins of Political Stability in England, 1675–1725*, Boston, 1967, pp. 27–8, 34–8; T. Hobbes, *Behemoth*, ed. F. Tonnies, London, 1889, pp. 43, 40; see also pp. 23, 56, 58, 155; L. Stone, 'Literacy and education in England, 1640–1900', *Past and Present*, 42, 1969, pp. 98–102.

121 I. K. Fierabend, A. L. Fierabend and B. A. Neswold, 'Social change and political violence', in *Violence in America: Historical and Comparative Perspectives*, ed. H. G. Graham and T. R. Gurr, Washington, 1969, 2, p. 524.

122 C. Hill, *The Intellectual Origins of the English Revolution*, Oxford, 1965, ch. 5; W. S. Holdsworth, op. cit., ch. 5, pp. 423–493; W. J. Jones, *The Elizabethan Court of Chancery*, Oxford, 1967, Part 3, *passim*.

123 P. Seaver, op. cit., p. 8.

124 J. F. Davis, 'Lollard survival and the textile industry in the south-east of England', *Studies in Church History*, 3, 1966; C. Hill, *Society and Puritanism in Pre-Revolutionary England*, London, 1964, ch. 4.

125 H. C. Porter, *Reformation and Reaction in Tudor Cambridge*, Cambridge, 1958, pp. 142–3.

126 C. Cross, *The Puritan Earl*, London, 1966, pp. 51, 138; P. Heylyn, *Historical and Miscellaneous Tracts*, London, 1681, p. 539 (quoted by C. Hill, *God's Englishman*, op. cit., p. 217). The best analysis of the relationship of Puritan theology to revolutionary practice is to be found in Hill, op. cit., ch. 9.

127 T. Hobbes, op. cit., p. 21.

128 W. Lamont, 'Puritanism as history and historiography', *Past and Present*, 44, 1969, pp. 137–46.

129 J. F. Wilson, *Pulpit in Parliament*, Princeton, 1969, pp. 224–235; L. B. Smith, 'English treason trials in the sixteenth century', *Journal of History of Ideas*, 15, 1954.

130 *A Century of Sermons . . . by John Hacket*, op. cit., p. xliii.

131 M. Walzer, *The Revolution of the Saints*, Cambridge, Mass., 1965, chs. 4, 5, 7; 'Puritanism as a revolutionary ideology', *History and Theory*, 3, 1963; J. E. Neale, *The Elizabethan House of Commons*, op. cit., p. 251; *Elizabeth I and her Parliaments*, op. cit., 2, 1957, p. 141; P. Collinson, *The Elizabethan Puritan Movement*, pp. 278–9, 303–6.

132 C. Hill, *Economic Problems of the Church*, pp. 252–67; A. P. Newton, *The Colonising Activities of the English Puritans*, New Haven, 1914, ch. 10.

133 J. G. A. Pococke, *The Ancient Law and the Feudal Constitution*, Cambridge, 1957, chs. 2, 3; C. Ogilvie, op. cit.; M. Judson, op. cit., ch. 2; E. W. Ives, 'Social change and the law', in his *The English Revolution, 1600–1660*, London, 1968.

134 W. Prest, 'Legal education of the gentry at the Inns of Court, 1560–1640', *Past and Present*, 38, 1967. Clarendon certainly assumed that a gentleman would pick up some law at the Inns (Edward Hyde, Earl of Clarendon, *Collection of Several Tracts*, London, 1727, pp. 327–30).

135 E. W. Ives, op. cit., p. 126.

136 P. Zagorin, *The Court and the Country*, op. cit., ch. 3.

137 H. F. Kearney, op. cit. p. 43.

138 J. G. A. Pococke, 'Machiavelli, Harrington, and English political ideologies in the eighteenth century', *William and Mary Quarterly*, 3rd ser., 22, 1965, p. 565.

139 J. Donne, *Poems*, ed. J. C. Grierson, London, 1912, pp. 237–238.

140 C. Hill, op. cit., ch. 3, and the articles and notes by several scholars in *Past and Present*, 28–31, 1964–5.

141 T. K. Rabb, 'Francis Bacon and the reform of society', in *Action and Conviction in Early Modern Europe*, ed. T. K. Rabb and J. E. Seigel, Princeton, 1970; H. R. Trevor-Roper, *Religion, the Reformation and Social Change*, London, 1967, pp. 257–8; B. J. Shapiro, 'Latitudinarism and science in seventeenth century England', *Past and Present*, 40, 1968.

142 M. de Certeau, 'L'histoire religieuse du XVIIe siècle: problèmes de methodes,' *Recherches de science religieuse*, 57 (no. 2), 1969, pp. 233–4.

143 C. Hill, op. cit., p. 8.

144 C. A. Holmes, 'The Eastern Association', Cambridge Ph.D. thesis, 1969, App. III, p. 495. I am grateful to Professor Holmes for permission to quote from his thesis. A. Everitt, *The Community of Kent and the Great Rebellion, 1640–60*, op. cit., p. 36; 'Suffolk and the Great Rebellion, 1640–1660', *Suffolk Record Society*, 3, 1960, p. 20; *Change in the*

Provinces: the 17th Century, Leicester, 1969, p. 38; J. T. Cliffe, *The Yorkshire Gentry*, London, 1969, p. 13.

145 R. H. Tawney, 'The rise of the gentry, 1558–1640', in E. M. Carus-Wilson, op. cit., 1, p. 192; Stone, *The Crisis of the Aristocracy*, op. cit. p. 157.

146 P. Laslett, 'Clayworth and Cogenhoe', in *Historical Essays, 1600–1750*, ed. H. E. Bell and R. L. Ollard, London, 1963, p. 177; E. A. Wrigley, 'London's importance, 1650–1750', *Past and Present*, 37, 1967, p. 46; E. E. Rich, 'The population of Elizabethan England', *Economic History Review*, 2nd ser., 2, 1950, pp. 258–65; L. Stone, 'Social mobility in England', op. cit., pp. 31–2; J. Cornwall, 'Evidence of population mobility in the seventeenth century', *Bulletin of the Institute for Historical Research*, 40, 1967, pp. 147, 150; D. Glass, 'Socio-economic status and occupations in the city of London at the end of the seventeenth century', *Studies in London History*, ed. A. E. J. Hollaender and W. Kellaway, London, 1969, pp. 386–7; V. H. T. Skipp, 'Economic and social change in the Forest of Arden, 1530–1649', *Agricultural History Review*, 18, Suppl., p. 108.

147 A. Everitt, *Change in the Provinces*, op. cit., p. 30.

148 D. M. Barrett, op. cit., p. 50.

149 M. Curtis, 'The alienated intellectuals of early Stuart England', *Past and Present*, 23, 1962.

150 J. E. Neale, 'The Commons' privilege of free speech in parliament', *Tudor Studies Presented to A. F. Pollard*, ed. R. W. Seton-Watson, London, 1924, p. 286.

151 E. Rogers, *Life and Opinions of a Fifth Monarchy Man*, London, 1867, pp. 49. (I owe this reference to Mr Peter Thon.)

152 H. R. Trevor-Roper, *Archbishop Laud, 1573–1645*, London, 1940; C. Hill, *The Economic Problems of the Church*, op. cit.

153 *The Works of William Laud*, ed. W. Scott and J. Bliss, Oxford, 1847–60, 5, Part 2, p. 499.

154 J. F. Wilson, *Pulpit in Parliament*, Princeton, 1969, p. 32; P. Seaver, op. cit., p. 254; *Past and Present*, 23, 1962, p. 36.

155 F. B. Williams, 'The Laudian Imprimatur', *The Library*, 5th ser., 15, 1960, p. 97.

156 *The History of the Troubles and Tryal of William Laud*, London, 1695, pp. 525–66.

157 G. Albion, *Charles I and the Court of Rome*, London, 1935, ch. 14. *Cal. S. P. Dom., 1640*, pp. 493, 38. Ten years later Hobbes repeated this judgment on the fatal results of this 'most effectual calumny' (Hobbes, op. cit., p. 60).

158 J. Rushworth, *Historical Collections, 1618–29*, 1, 1682, p. 225.

159 F. C. Dietz, *English Public Finance, 1558–1641*, New York, 1932, pp. 262–8, 303; M. J. Hawkins, 'Sales of Wards in Somerset, 1603–41', *Somerset Rec. Soc.*, 67, 1965, pp. xxii–xxiii; G. Hammersley, 'The revival of the forest laws under Charles I', *History*, 45, 1960.

160 L. Stone, *The Crisis of the Aristocracy*, op. cit., pp. 119–28, 424–8.

161 R. Ashton, *The Crown and the Money Market, 1603–1640*, Oxford, 1960, ch. 4.

162 J. P. Kenyon, *The Stuart Constitution*, Cambridge, 1966, p. 86.

163 T. G. Barnes, op. cit., pp. 299–309.

164 V. F. Snow, 'Essex and the aristocratic opposition to the Early Stuarts', *Journal of Modern History*, 32, 1960.

165 Stone, *The Crisis of the Aristocracy*, op. cit., pp. 34, 117–19, 397–8, 751.

166 G. Unwin, *Industrial Organization in the Sixteenth and Seventeenth Centuries*, Oxford, 1904, pp. 142–71; V. Pearl, *London and the Outbreak of the Puritan Revolution*, Oxford, 1961, pp. 79–91; R. Ashton, 'Cavaliers and Capitalists', *Renaissance and Modern Studies*, 5, 1961, pp. 165–8; R. Ashton, 'Charles I and the City', *Essays in the Economic and Social History of Tudor and Stuart England*, op. cit.

167 G. D. Ramsay, *The Wiltshire Woollen Industry*, London, 1943, ch. 6.

168 R. H. Tawney, 'The rise of the gentry', op. cit., p. 203.

169 H. R. Trevor-Roper, 'Archbishop Laud', *History*, 30, 1945; G. Aylmer, *The King's Servants*, pp. 193–201; 'Office holding as factor in English history, 1625–42', *History*, 44, 1959; J. S. Wilson, 'Sir Henry Spelman and the Royal Commission on Fees', *Studies Presented to Sir Hilary Jenkinson*, London, 1957.

170 R. Howell, *Newcastle upon Tyne and the Puritan Revolution*, op. cit., chs. 2, 3; V. Pearl, op. cit., ch. 3; R. Ashton 'Charles I and the City', op. cit.

171 R. Ashton, *The Crown and the Money Market*, pp. 182–3.

172 I owe this paragraph to Dr N. R. N. Tyacke, 'Arminianism in religion and politics, 1604–40', D.Phil. thesis, Oxford, 1968.

173 P. Seaver, op. cit., p. 65.

174 H. E. I. Phillips, 'The last years of Star Chamber', *Transactions of the Royal Historical Society*, 4th ser., 21.

175 I owe my knowledge of Warwick's activities to Mr Christopher Thompson. J. H. Plumb, 'The Growth of the

Electorate in England, 1600–1715', *Past and Present*, 45, 1969.

176 E. J. Hobsbawm, 'The crisis of the seventeenth century', in *Crisis in Europe, 1560–1660*, op. cit.; B. Supple, *Commercial Crisis and Change in England, 1600–1642*, Cambridge, 1964, Part 1, chs. 3–6.

177 W. G. Hoskins, 'Harvest fluctuations and English economic history, 1620–1759', *Agricultural History Review*, 16, 1968, pp. 17, 20.

178 E. Kerridge, 'The movement of rent, 1540–1640', *Economic History Review*, 2nd ser., 6, 1953; L. Stone, *The Crisis of the Aristocracy*, op. cit., pp. 324–34.

179 T. Ranger, 'Strafford in Ireland: a revaluation', *Past and Present*, 19, 1961.

180 I owe the information about peers to Mr W. S. Schumacher; D. Brunton and D. H. Pennington, *Members of the Long Parliament*, London, 1954, p. 188; A. Everitt, *The Community of Kent and the Great Rebellion, 1640–1660*, op. cit., p. 118; S. C. Newton, 'The gentry of Derbyshire in the seventeenth century', *Derbyshire Archaeol. Soc. Trans.*, 86, 1966, p. 4.

181 H. F. Kearney, *Scholars and Gentlemen*, pp. 91–6.

182 Chalmers Johnson, *Revolutionary Change*, Boston, 1966, p. xiv.

183 T. L. Moir, *The Addled Parliament of 1614*, Oxford, 1958, pp. 56–7; M. F. Keeler, *The Long Parliament*, Philadelphia, 1954, p. 23; L. Stone, 'The electoral influence of the 2nd Earl of Salisbury', *English Historical Review*, 1956, pp. 390–1; J. H. Plumb, op. cit., p. 107.

184 J. K. Greenfelder, 'The Election to the Short Parliament' in *Early Stuart Studies*, ed. H. S. Reinmuth, Minneapolis, 1970, pp. 191–2, 184, 204, 217, 219.

185 J. F. Wilson, *Pulpit in Parliament, passim*. For the functions of ideology, see C. Geertz, 'Ideology as a cultural system', in D. Apter, *Ideology and Discontent*, New York, 1964.

186 S. Marshall, *Meroz Cursed*, London, 1641, pp. 10–12.

187 A. Heimert, *Religion and the American Mind*, Cambridge, Mass., 1966, ch. 9.

188 V. Pearl, op. cit., p. 127.

189 C. Hill, *The Century of Revolution*, op. cit., p. 121.

190 J. P. Kenyon, *The Stuart Constitution*, Cambridge, 1966, p. 2, n. 1.

191 A. S. P. Woodhouse, *Puritanism and Liberty*, London, 1938, p. 234; R. P. Brenner, 'Commercial Change and Political Conflict: The Merchant Community in Civil War London', Ph.D. thesis, Princeton University, 1970, pp. 372–3.

192 J. T. Cliffe, op. cit., ch. 15. I have reworked Dr Cliffe's figures in this and the following statements.

193 *Calendar of Committee for Compounding with Delinquents*, pp. 1558. See also pp. 897, 985, 1497.

194 I owe this information to Mr W. S. Schumacher.

195 *Hist. MSS. Commission*, 7th Report, p. 440.

196 For example, the estrangement between Sir Edmund Verney and his son Sir Ralph (*Memoirs of the Verney Family during the Seventeenth Century*, ed. F. R. and M. M. Verney, London, 1907, I, p. 255).

197 I owe this information to an unpublished paper by Professor R. P. Brenner.

198 A. S. Butler, 'A Letter from Mercurius Civicus to Mercurius Rusticus', *Somers Tracts*, ed. W. Scott, 1810, IV, p. 598.

199 C. Hill, *Puritanism and Revolution*, op. cit., p. 152.

200 C. Robbins, *The Eighteenth Century Commonwealthman*, Cambridge, Mass., 1959.

Index

Index

dysfunction, 9, 10, 114

Eckstein, Harry, 8, 9, 11, 12, 23
education and educational institutions, xii, 74, 114, 116–17, 147; elementary, 96; grammar schools, 66, 95, 97; universities, 66, 95, 96, 113
Edward I, 51
Edward VI, 64
elections and electorate, 96, 130, 135, 136, 147
Eliot, Sir John, 130
Elizabeth I, 27, 58, 60, 61, 66, 77–82 *passim*, 85–92 *passim*, 94, 102, 115–16
emigration, 120
Engels, Friedrich, 39, 40, 43, 47, 148, 150
Essex, Robert Devereux, 2nd Earl, 85
Essex, Robert Devereux, 3rd Earl, 124, 142, 144

Filmer, Robert, 91
Foxe, John, 88

Gardiner, S. R., 26, 47, 148, 149, 150
gentry, 27–31 *passim*, 33, 51, 55–6, 63, 69, 72–3, 75, 92, 95, 98, 99, 104, 106, 108, 112, 113, 116, 120, 122, 123, 124, 125, 129, 130, 131, 141–2, 143; income, 73–4; 'mere gentry', 27, 28, 35, 47–8, 55, 143; transfer of manors, 110, 154
George III, 140
Gottschalk, Louis, 3, 9, 23
government: central, xii, 48, 57, 136; local, xii, 63–4, 95
Grand Remonstrance, 70, 141
Gurr, T. R., 18, 19, 23

Hacket, John, Bishop, 103
Hakewill, William, 105
Halévy, Elie, 12
Hampden, John, 130
Harrington, James, 35, 38–9, 48, 148
Hartlib, Samuel, 52, 109
Hastings, Sir Francis, 100
Henrietta Maria, Queen, 121, 127, 142
Henry II, 51
Henry VII, 58, 59
Henry VIII, 51, 58, 59, 64, 65, 66, 75, 78, 88
Herbert, Edward, Lord, 58–9, 150
Hexter, J. H., 28–9, 31, 35, 36, 40–3

passim, 148, 150
Hill, J. E. C., 28, 32, 36, 40–3 *passim*, 47, 148, 149, 150, 152, 155, 159, 160, 163, 164
Hobbes, Thomas, 38, 49, 51, 53, 96, 101, 149, 159, 161
Hooker, Richard, 81
Hopper, Rex D., 21

'internal war', 4–6, 12, 23
Ireton, Henry, 105
Irish Rebellion, 137–8, 139

James I, 27, 61, 78, 79, 81, 83, 89–90, 92–5 *passim*, 104, 158
James II, 134
'J-curve', 15, 16, 17, 19, 125, 131
Johnson, Chalmers, xiv, 6, 7, 9, 10–11, 22, 23, 135, 163
Jones, Inigo, 106
Justices of the Peace, 72, 95, 104, 107, 124, 132
Juxon, William, Bishop, 119

Kett, Robert, 6
King, *see* Crown and monarchy
King, Gregory, 75
Klng, Merle, 3
Knollys, Hanserd, 142

Labrousse, C. E., 16
Latimer, Hugh, Bishop, 88
Laud, William, Archbishop, 51, 83, 101, 112, 118, 120, 121, 127–35 *passim*, 137
law and legislature, 62–3, 71, 75, 102–3; courts, 62, 71, 97; lawyers, 75, 104–5, 112, 114, 151, 160; Star Chamber, 129; test cases, 94, 97, 104; *see also* Justices of the Peace
Leicester, Robert Sidney, Earl, 96
Lenin, Nikolai, xiv
Lenski, G. E., 19, 24, 150
Levellers, 48, 49, 50, 57, 97, 103
Lewis, Sir Arthur, 14, 15, 16, 24
Locke, John, 105, 147
London, 70–1, 111, 119, 127, 128, 135, 140, 145; trading companies, 127–8
Louis XVI, 11, 20
Ludlow, Edmund, 141
Lunsford, Sir Thomas, 138
Lyly, John, 88

Macaulay, Thomas Babington, 47, 148

Index

Marshall, Stephen, 139–40
Marx, Karl, and Marxism, xii, 7, 14, 17, 26, 36, 38, 39, 47, 54
Mary, Queen, 64
Mary, Queen of Scots, 78
Mathijs, John, 6
Maynard, Sir John, 136
merchants, 55, 75, 112, 114, 127, 144–5
Merton, Robert, 14
Middleton, Thomas, 69
Milton, John, 90
monarchy, *see* Crown and monarchy
Moore, Wilbert, 10
More, Sir Thomas, 39, 43

Namier, Sir Lewis, 29
Nasser, Gamal, 7
Neumann, Sigmund, 23, 48, 148
Newcastle, William Cavendish, Duke, 90, 91
Nixon, Richard, 79
nobility, 51, 63, 99, 125, 142, 143
Northumberland, Henry Percy, Earl, 142, 144

Oakes, Urian, 83
Olson, Moncur, 14, 15, 16, 24

pamphleteering, 49–50, 66, 137
Parker, Henry, 53, 129, 149
Parliament, xii, 52–3, 59, 76, 87, 90, 108, 122, 123–4, 132, 135–6; House of Commons, 29, 38, 63, 91–3, 95, 115–16, 124, 129, 133, 138–9; House of Lords, 29, 48, 49, 51, 124, 133, 146, 147; Long Parliament, 55, 104, 126, 136, 137; Short Parliament, 136
Parliamentarians, 34, 53, 56, 133, 143
Parsons, Talcott, 14, 24
Pembroke, Philip Herbert, 4th Earl, 144
Pennington, D. H., 32, 42
Pettee, George S., 3, 8, 23
poor, 54–5, 147
population, 67, 76
Prynne, William, 50, 105, 130
Pugachev, Yemelyan I., 6
Puritans and Puritanism, 13, 30, 47, 50, 51, 58, 82, 95–104 *passim*, 108, 109, 115, 116, 128, 137, 145, 159; lecturers and preachers, 90, 103, 113–14, 120–1, 139; political consequences, 100–3

Pym, John, 52, 109, 130, 138, 140–3 *passim*

Raleigh, Sir Walter, 89
reference-group theory, 18
relative deprivation, 18, 20, 134
revolution: causes, 8–20; definitions and types, 3–8; groups, 13; social stages, 20–2; special factors in, 10–11; theories of, 3–25
Rostow, W. W., 16, 24
Royalists, 34, 35, 56, 133, 140–4 *passim*
Rupert, Prince, 142

Salisbury, James Cecil, Earl, 136, 142, 144
Salisbury, Robert Cecil, Earl, 83
Sandys, Edwin, Archbishop, 80
Savonarola, Girolamo, 6
Saye and Sele, William Fiennes, Viscount, 130, 144
scepticism, 108–9
Seldenr, John, 80, 121
Shklar, J., 35, 43
Sibbes, Richard, 99
social mobility, 110–12, 113
Stapleton, Sir Robert, 80
Stone, Lawrence, ix, 27, 29, 36, 41, 42, 151, 153–9 *passim*, 161, 162
Strafford, Thomas Wentworth, Earl, 128, 130, 131, 132, 133, 138, 141
Supple, Barry, 16, 24, 153

Tawney, R. H., 26, 27, 28, 31, 32, 35, 36, 40, 41, 42, 47, 148, 150, 153, 161, 162
taxes and taxation, 60–1, 62, 77, 85, 115, 122, 123, 132, 136, 155; ship money, 62, 122, 134
'Thorough', 126, 127, 135
Tilly, Charles, 15
Tocqueville, Alexis de, 14, 16, 84
trade and industry, 99, 110; cloth, 68–9, 70, 131; coal, 70; internal, 69; overseas, 68–9; rural, 71
Trevelyan, G. M., 31, 42, 148
Trevor-Roper, H. R., 27–8, 31, 35–8 *passim*, 40, 41, 43, 47, 148, 149, 161, 162
Tyndale, William, 88

Underdown, D., 33, 42

Van Dyck, Sir Anthony, 106